The Top Ten Guide to Fly Fishing

Jay Zimmerman

Illustrations by Kendall Zimmerman

LYONS PRESS
Guilford, Connecticut
An imprint of Globe Pequot Press

Lyons Press is an imprint of Globe Pequot Press.

All photos by Jay Zimmerman unless otherwise noted.

Project editor: Meredith Dias
Text design and layout: Sue Murray

Library of Congress Cataloging-in-Publication Data

Zimmerman, Jay.
  The top ten guide to fly fishing / Jay Zimmerman ; illustrations by Kendall Zimmerman.
    p. cm.
  Includes index.
  ISBN 978-0-7627-8224-6
  1. Fly fishing—United States—Handbooks, manuals, etc. I. Title. II. Title: Guide to fly fishing.
  SH456.Z56 2013
  799.12'4—dc23
                                                                      2012026493

Printed in the United States of America

10 9 8 7 6 5 4 3 2 1

Contents

Foreword xiii

Chapter 1
The Top Ten Things to Look for When Selecting a New Fly Rod..... 1

   10. Filling a Void 2
    9. Old School vs. New School 3
    8. Price Tag 4
    7. The Specs 4
    6. Kicking the Tires 5
    5. Model vs. Brand 6
    4. Sweet Spots 6
    3. Package Deals 7
    2. Made in America 7
    1. The Fine Print 8

Chapter 2
The Top Ten Things to Look for When Selecting a New Fly Reel 9

   10. Capacity 9
    9. Price Points 10
    8. Machined vs. Cast 10
    7. Warranty 11
    6. Drag 12
    5. Arbor Size 12
    4. Weight and Color 13
    3. Made in the USA 14
    2. Brand 14
    1. Spare Spools 15

Chapter 3
The Top Ten Things to Look for
When Selecting a New Fly Line and Leader

When Selecting a New Fly Line and Leader 17
10. Weight Forward vs. Double Taper...............................17
 9. Freshwater vs. Saltwater...19
 8. Sinking Line 19
 7. Over-Lining 20
 6. Furled Leaders 20
 5. Long Leaders vs. Short Leaders 21
 4. Nylon vs. Fluorocarbon 21
 3. Brand 22
 2. Maintenance...22
 1. When to Replace 23

Chapter 4
The Top Ten Things to Look for
When Selecting New Boots and Waders

When Selecting New Boots and Waders 25
10. The Warranty...25
 9. Buying Online..27
 8. High-End vs. Low-End...27
 7. Stocking-Foot Tales..28
 6. A Whole Lot of Frontal..28
 5. The Seams...29
 4. Size Matters..30
 3. The Sole Issue 30
 2. Underneath It All 31
 1. Maintaining Your Stuff..32

Chapter 5
The Top Ten Fly-Fishing Accessories

The Top Ten Fly-Fishing Accessories 33
10. Magnetic Net Release 33
 9. Fly Threader 33
 8. LED Headlamp...34
 7. Split-Shot Dispenser 34

6. Versatile Fly Box 35
5. Tippet Spool Tender 35
4. Soft Cooler 37
3. Polarized Sunglasses 37
2. A Good Map 38
1. Off/Mute Button on Cell Phone 39

Chapter 6
The Top Ten Ways to Get What You Need at a Fly Shop 41

10. Do Some Homework 41
9. Know Their Names 42
8. Help Me Help You...42
7. Talk to Your Guide..43
6. Red Flags 43
5. Be Prepared to Get Information...44
4. Common Courtesy...45
3. Don't Be a Vulture 45
2. Be Open to Suggestion...46
1. Beer..46

Chapter 7
The Top Ten Ways to Save Money in Fly Fishing 47

10. Fish Local 47
9. Tie Your Own Flies...48
8. Build Leaders from Scratch 48
7. Dry Your Fly Boxes 49
6. Take Care of Your Glasses 49
5. Take Care of Your Fly Line 49
4. Take Care of Your Waders 51
3. Buy It to Turn It 51
2. Pack a Lunch 52
1. Organize...52

Chapter 8

The Top Ten Must-Know Knots and Rigging Techniques 53
  10. Reel and Line 53
   9. Leader to Tippet 57
   8. Tippet to Fly 57
   7. Lake vs. River 59
   6. Single Dry Fly 61
   5. Dry and Dropper 61
   4. Indicator Nymphing 62
   3. High-Stick Nymphing..62
   2. Euro-Nymphing..63
   1. Streamer and Wet Fly Fishing 64

Chapter 9

The Top Ten Ways to Improve Your Fishing 67
  10. Get in Shape...67
   9. Learn to Tie 68
   8. The Long Rod 68
   7. Partner Up..68
   6. Document the Day 69
   5. Attention to Detail 69
   4. Cross Train...70
   3. Fish Harder...70
   2. Fish Smarter 72
   1. Fish Places Others Don't 72

Chapter 10

The Top Ten Tricks of the Trade 73
  10. The Tuber Hatch 73
   9. Dealing with Ducks 74
   8. Dealing with Other Anglers 75
   7. Fishing with a Partner...75

6. The Things That Scare Fish 77
5. Setting the Hook 78
4. Nymphers Do It Deeper 79
3. Become a Thief..80
2. Locked and Loaded..80
1. One Shot, One Kill..80

Chapter 11
The Top Ten Rules of Etiquette 81
10. Show Up on Time...81
9. Hot Spotting..81
8. Boat Culture..82
7. Catch-and-Release 83
6. Exaggerated Reporting..83
5. Barbless Hooks 84
4. Redd Raiding...84
3. Give Others Space 85
2. Be a Steward...85
1. Respect the Fish 85

Chapter 12
The Top Ten Ways to Improve Your Casting...............................89
10. It's All in the Wrist 90
9. Lack of Authority 90
8. Use Your Rod..91
7. Out of Sight, Out of Mind...91
6. Line Pickup 91
5. Take a Bow...92
4. Line Speed..92
3. Letting Go 93
2. Over Casting 93
1. Change It Up 94

Chapter 13
The Top Ten Mistakes Made by Novices 95
   10. The Casting Issue 96
    9. Poor Preparation..96
    8. Not Reading vs. Reading Too Much 97
    7. Bad Advice 97
    6. Gadgets...98
    5. In Over Your Head 98
    4. Fear of Knots...98
    3. Time on the Water...99
    2. Being a Bad Dancer..99
    1. The Wrong Attitude...100

Chapter 14
The Top Ten Ways to Take Better Fishing Photos 101
   10. Preparation 102
    9. Stop and Poke at Bugs 102
    8. Postcard Moments 103
    7. Bent Rods 103
    6. Remove Those Sunglasses 104
    5. Fill Flash 104
    4. The Money Shot 104
    3. More Spots, Less Knuckles 105
    2. Don't Forget the Fish...105
    1. And . . . the Release! 106

Chapter 15
The Top Ten Trout Dry Flies.....................................107
   10. Stimulator 107
    9. Clown Shoe Caddis 107
    8. Amy's Ant...108
    7. RS2...109
    6. Missing Link 109

5. Curmudgeon Crumpler 109
4. Comparadun 110
3. Beetle 111
2. Elk Hair Caddis 111
1. Parachute Adams 111

Chapter 16
The Top Ten Trout Nymphs 113
10. Girdle Bug 113
9. Copper John 114
8. Banksia Bug 114
7. Rainbow Warrior 114
6. Jujubaetis 115
5. Prince 116
4. Zebra Midge 117
3. Micro May 117
2. Two-Bit Hooker 117
1. Pheasant Tail 118

Chapter 17
The Top Ten Trout Streamers 119
10. Gray Ghost 119
9. Autumn Splendor 120
8. Sculpzilla 120
7. Platte River Spider 121
6. Sparkle Minnow 122
5. Near Nuff Sculpin 122
4. Belly Ache Minnow 123
3. Woolly Bugger 124
2. Muddler Minnow 124
1. Pine Squirrel Leech 125

Chapter 18
The Top Ten Warm-Water Flies 127
   10. Flashtail Whistler 128
    9. Geezus Lizard 128
    8. Charlie's Airhead 128
    7. Backstabber 129
    6. Meat Whistle 129
    5. Near Nuff Crayfish 129
    4. Booby Frog 130
    3. Texas Ringworm 131
    2. Dahlberg's Diver 131
    1. Clouser Minnow 132

Chapter 19
The Top Ten Saltwater Flies 135
   10. Reducer 135
    9. Chili Pepper Worm 136
    8. Megalopsicle 136
    7. Crazy Charlie 137
    6. Reefer Mantis 137
    5. Crease Fly 138
    4. Clouser Minnow 138
    3. Del's Merkin Crab 139
    2. Gotcha 139
    1. Lefty's Deceiver 139

Chapter 20
The Top Ten Alaskan Streamers 141
   10. Polar Shrimp 141
    9. Green Butt Skunk 142
    8. Boss 143
    7. Killawatte 143

6. Articulated Leech 143
5. Supervisor 144
4. Flesh Fly..144
3. Alaskabou 145
2. Egg-Sucking Leech...146
1. Flash Fly 147

Chapter 21
The Top Ten Beginning Tying Patterns......................149
10. Annelids 149
9. Midge Pupae 150
8. Scuds and Sow Bugs 150
7. PTs and Hare's Ears 151
6. Ashers and Gnats 151
5. Beetles and Ants...152
4. Para-Mayflies 152
3. Elk Hair Caddis 152
2. Leeches...153
1. Woolly Buggers 154

Chapter 22
The Top Ten Fly-Tying Tricks 155
10. The Right Equipment 156
9. Get Yourself Organized 157
8. Heavy Thread 157
7. Do Your Chores...158
6. Cheap Charlie 158
5. Avoid the Witches' Brew 159
4. The Best Parts Are Body Parts...............................159
3. Garbage Bag Bears 160
2. Be a Good Closer 161
1. Bathtub Testing...161

Contents

Chapter 23

The Top Ten Destinations in the United States............................163

   10. Bozeman, Montana...163

    9. Cape Cod, Massachusetts 164

    8. Guntersville, Alabama...165

    7. Hayward, Wisconsin 166

    6. Key Largo, Florida 166

    5. Kodiak, Alaska..168

    4. Lander, Wyoming...169

    3. Maupin, Oregon...169

    2. New Orleans, Louisana 170

    1. Steamboat Springs, Colorado 171

Acknowledgments 172

Index...173

About the Author 178

Foreword

We've all walked into fly shops (especially when we're new to the sport) and had the distinct feeling of being out of the loop. The club is meeting and we somehow missed the memo—or maybe we weren't supposed to get the memo. There's always that possibility, too. But this book is, if you will, that memo. It's the accumulated knowledge of experience, written down to get you in the loop.

Jay Zimmerman might have been born with a fly rod in his hands, I don't know (more likely, it was a recurve bow), but this book strikes me as all the things he wishes he'd known when he was starting out, with trial and error his teachers on the streams and ponds of his native Ohio. And even if you have been fly fishing for a while, Jay delivers the unique perspective of one who has worked in the industry—as a guide and in a fly shop—for almost a decade. For example, he will tell you *how to get what you want in a fly shop,* from his behind-the-counter point of view.

Having written on the subject for a number of years, as well as having read many how-to books, articles, and blog posts—admittedly, most of them are horribly dry (think day-old bakery bread, and add a cough just for effect)—I enjoy the ones that surprise me with a laugh or tell a story at the same time. And Jay has a knack for both of these. His good humor, pragmatism, and command of the ever-elusive common sense combine with the ability to write and instruct as an organic whole (which you will see in the following pages). This book is a little wit, a little history, a little practicality. Plus, Jay has retained the memory of what it was like to not know how to tie a Rapala knot, what a Muddler is, or how to choose between weight-forward or double-tapered lines. So this book jumps to no conclusions or eager acronyms, and its uniqueness lies therein. Even beginners will understand every principle presented; yet the advanced fisherman will learn something, too, or will at least come to think about something in a new way. Ethics, perhaps? Or something as simple as being reminded to take off one's sunglasses before gripping and grinning.

The one word you'll hear again and again about Jay is "approachable"—and I can say with full confidence that his writing can be described as the same. And through reading this book, you'll walk through that metaphorical fly shop door and feel comfortable, with him standing behind the counter giving you a welcoming nod and g'day. And if you read with your ears open, you'll come out of this book—out of this "fly shop"—a much better and more knowledgeable fisherman than when you went in.

Erin Block
Mysteries Internal

Chapter 1

The Top Ten Things to Look for When Selecting a New Fly Rod

Anyone who has ever made a living working in or running or owning a fly shop will eventually feel like a career waiter. A high school kid with a haircut can make a decent waiter, or if he's nuts about fly fishing, can land a minimum wage gig working the sales floor of a local shop. What separates this kid   although he may be

Randy Hicks displays a giant brown trout. Sometimes a 4-weight rod won't cut it. Eric DeCaria

well-meaning—and a veteran shop rat is his knowledge of the tools of the sport and his ability to peg a potential customer. Many of those in the market for a new fly rod enter a fly shop attempting to be as cool and nonchalant as they can, even if they have only been borrowing friends' equipment up until that moment. A good shop employee will conduct a very nonthreatening interrogation of sorts to best assess the way to proceed. This chapter is not broken down in order of importance, but in chronological order of what questions will be asked. To keep with the premise and outline of this book, I will begin with point number 10.

10: Filling a Void

The first thing I try to figure out is whether you are in my fly shop to replace a rod. Maybe you broke your favorite 4-weight and it didn't have a warranty, or maybe a guide knocked it out of a drift boat with an errant oar ("Sorry . . . guess we'll just count that as the tip!"), or maybe you are finally ready to upgrade from that lazy noodle you were gifted fifteen years ago. This is easy. You *had* a 9-foot 4-weight, you want *another* 9-foot 4-weight. But, if it is not just a mere replacement, things get a bit trickier. Now you are attempting to fill a void, and I have to know what rods you already have and what you do with them—and what you hope to gain with the purchase of a new one. Often I will ask a fisherman to describe the last time he was on the water and felt ill-equipped. Was the rod too soft? Did it not have enough power to cast a large streamer into the wind? Or was it too long and clunky to wield on your favorite small creek? Does it not allow the 8-inch brookies room to show off? It is always best to put some thought into this before you start casting random rods and searching for an excuse to buy something. Also, if this is going to be your very first fly rod, be honest with yourself: Where do you foresee fishing the most in this, your first year into the sport? I recommend it be your home water—the best fishing with the shortest drive time. Again, put some thought into this so you have a ready answer when asked. The guy at your local fly shop will be able to hand you the perfect tool for the job. After all, *it is his home water, too!*

9: Old School vs. New School

This is not a subject that comes up very often in fly shops anymore, but I am always prepared to give a brief crash course on fly rod construction and materials—usually the shorter the course the better, so as not to bore away potential consumerism. There was a time in this country when every fly rod was made from six triangular split slivers of bamboo. These six pieces were glued together to form a hexagonal two- or three-piece rod blank that was assembled using slim metal ferrules. There were hundreds of manufacturers cranking out these heavy, slow-action arm busters in the 1950s. So, if you find one of these rods in your grandfather's attic, don't get too excited: It is likely as worthless as his baseball card collection. However, always keep an eye out for a Ted Williams or Mickey Mantel with good corners, or a Granger or Phillipson with both tips and the original tube! But I digress. So, in the post–World War II industrial boom, we were introduced to many new gadgets and improvements in the fishing industry—spinning reels, rubber waders, and fiberglass fly rods, to name just three. The new fiberglass rods had the same slow action as bamboo and usually came in two pieces and with metal ferrules, but were much lighter weight and more durable, not to mention far faster to produce. Many of these fly rods, if properly taken care of, are still perfectly functional and enjoyable fishing tools—some modern rod manufacturers still offer fiberglass models in their line. But then came the 1970s and the age of the graphite fly rod . . . much lighter and much faster. If you walk into a fly shop these days, there is a good chance every rod in the shop is made of graphite.

8: Price Tag

Yeah, it always comes down to cash money, so we may as well address it now. Fly rods can get very, very expensive. But, so can wine and sports cars. In the end it all depends on your taste and budget. You will be looking at over $700 for most of the high-end rods these days, but you can just as easily find a two-piece no-name for well under $100. Usually these low-end rods are cheaply and poorly built, carry no warranty, and can only be found at a big-box store (same aisle as the snelled hooks, three-way swivels, and salmon eggs). There are, however, an ever-increasing number of well-built rods made by reputable manufacturers that carry lifetime breakage warranties and don't cost as much as a used car. If you are looking for a great fly rod at a decent price, be prepared to spend between $150 and $350.

7: The Specs

A fly rod is not a "fishing pole," just as a fine hunting rifle is not a "gun." And, as there are rifles built for specific purposes (like a .30-30 for the brushy Midwest, a .22-250 for flat-shootin' varmints, or a good ol' .300 Win Mag for big game), there are specific lengths and weights of fly rods designed for particular situations. If I lost you with all that rifle waffle, then maybe golf clubs are a better analogy. Sure, you can play an entire eighteen holes with a 7 iron (Tin Cup did it with garden tools!), but there is good reason to lug around a bag full of irons and a sand wedge. When it comes to fly rod weights, it can be just as simple. I have seen fly rods go down as small as triple-0 and as high as 16-weight, but for all practical intents and purposes, you should stay somewhere between a 3-weight and a 10-weight rod. Generally the 3s and 4s are used for small to medium-size trout streams; 5s and 6s for lakes and larger rivers; 7s and 8s for bass, pike, and salmon; and, lastly, 9s and 10s are usually used for saltwater species such as bonefish, permit, tarpon, and roosterfish. Again, these are purely generalizations . . . there are always exceptions to these rules.

Then there is the rod length. I have heard it said (and I agree) that any fly rod had better have a good excuse for being under 8 feet or over 9. The trade-off is the ease of wielding a short rod under tree branches, and the advantage of a longer rod in reach and line control once the cast is made. This is partially the reason you will only see rods shorter than 9 feet in the lighter, small-stream 3- and 4-weights. On the other hand, if you are almost always fishing medium to large rivers with plenty of casting room, then *why not* carry a 10-foot 5-weight? It will give you incredible reach and fantastic drag-free drifts.

Finally, we should talk about how many pieces the rod breaks down to. More importantly, this should really be a conversation about how short the rod tube needs to be in order to be easy for you to carry around. *Four!* There, I answered the question, ended the conversation. A four-piece fly rod is what you want. You can strap two of them to a rucksack for a hike into the high country, stow them in the overhead bin of an airplane, or stash them behind the bench seat of your pickup. And, no, two-piece rods don't cast better than four-piece rods. You heard the sort of conjecture years ago: *There are dead spots where the ferrules are . . .* Not true anymore. The quality of the graphite used and the overall ferrule design have improved to the point that not even the best tournament fly casters can tell the difference.

6: Kicking the Tires

Never buy a fly rod without casting it first. There are many different rod actions out there, and although graphite rods are often broken down into three action categories (medium, medium-fast, and fast), each rod casts a little bit different than the next. You want to know what fits you the best, and there is only one way to find out. Have the guys at the fly shop pull out one of their demo reels from under the counter and string up. Heck, have them pick out three or four comparable rods for you to try. Besides, this is a great way to get a free casting lesson . . . Yes, swallow your ego and have a pro watch your cast. You may be amazed at what ten minutes and an open mind will get you.

5: Model vs. Brand

I get hit with the question about my favorite rod brand all the time. It is a fair question. Many of my customers have known and trusted me for years, and they want to know what I choose to fish with. Sure. But my answer has always been the outright denial of having any brand loyalties. I do have some serious model favorites, though, the difference being each fly rod manufacturer offers several different models in their lineup (usually somewhere between five and twelve), and they do their best to cover the entire spectrum of actions and preferences. And you have more than just a few rod companies. This can make your choice of a new rod more and more complicated and confusing the more research you do—*option paralysis*. But use this to your advantage as a consumer: Put in the work, cast the rods, and ask the right questions . . . There is a perfect rod for you out there.

4: Sweet Spots

This is more of a continuation of point number 5. We cannot have a thorough conversation about fly rod models without talking about sweet spots within a particular line. This sounds weird, I know, but most rod companies design a new rod model with one length and weight intended to be the "poster child." These companies will rarely admit this and never let on as to which one it is, so it is up to you, the caster, to figure it out. Keep in mind, this is something only advanced casters need to pay attention to. One easy way to narrow this down is to look at how that particular rod model is marketed: Is it primarily talked about as a precise, delicate rod and the stock catalog photos show a guy on a small spring creek in Pennsylvania? Sure, probably the best in the lineup is the 3- or 4-weight 7½- to 8½-footer. Is it being marketed as a powerful yet graceful lightweight casting tool and the manufacturer has website home page photos of a guy fishing some well-known river in Montana? Yup, most likely it is the 9-foot 5- or 6-weight they want you to cast. And if it is a rod model that is very deliberately targeting the saltwater crowd, then the 8- and 9-weights are the ones you should look at. Many of these heavy sticks are only offered in weights down to a 6—and that, too, should be an indicator. Be aware of the range of weights offered in the line, and focus on the middle of the pack.

3: Package Deals

Fly shops sell truckloads of preassembled rod-and-reel packages to beginners. This is not a bad thing—these setups are a great way to get into the sport for under $200. Most reputable fly rod manufacturers offer at least a couple of these packages, usually only in the most common of the lengths and weights. The upside to these package deals is the fly rod will often carry some sort of breakage warranty, being the highest-quality piece in the setup. The downside is the reel and everything else is usually a tad chintzy. But this is not always the end of the world. Say the reel and fly line only last you two seasons—by then you will be ready for a second, or maybe even a third, rod. And the rod in the package had a lifetime warranty, so that will be around for awhile . . . and the whole thing only cost you $180 anyway. *Nice!*

2: Made in America

Well, this one is simple: All the best fly rods are still made in the United States. However, these are usually the higher-end, expensive ones. Many rod manufacturers build most of their mid- to high-end stuff here in the USA, but contract the lower-end rods in their lineup out to China, Korea, or some other country that specializes in Research & Copy more than Research & Development. So, if this matters to you, ask someone in a fly shop that you trust (some shops will scrape the *Made in Korea* sticker off the butt end of all the rods!).

1: The Fine Print

I believe the word *warranty* has been mentioned at least a half-dozen times now, so we may as well address the topic. There is a fairly common misconception about how an Unconditional Lifetime Warranty on a fly rod is handled. Most rod companies will replace a broken rod (or just the broken section) no matter how the poor four-piece miraculously turned into a five- or six-piece. Some of the more common culprits are car doors, automatic car windows, temper tantrums, and bad casts with heavy streamers. All are covered under warranty. Lost rods or lost tip sections *are not* covered. The misunderstanding is how much the repair/replacement fee is. Sure, you won't have to buy a new rod, but you will have to pay between $35 and $50 (depending on the rod manufacturer) to get the replacement. You can go online to most fly rod company websites, print out a repair form, and get their repairs department address. Or, if you are lazy, you can usually take the busted rod down to your local fly shop and have them ship it out for you. Keep in mind that the turnaround time for most replaced rods is three to four weeks, and you can't expect the fly shop to send out your rod right away—or call you immediately once it returns. So, if it is urgent you have your rod back quickly, it may be best to send it in yourself. If you do decide to have your fly shop take care of it, expect to pay $10 or $20 for shipping.

Chapter 2

The Top Ten Things to Look for When Selecting a New Fly Reel

Fly fishing is a simple and primitive endeavor. Do your best to keep that in mind when you are gearing up. But it has turned into a rather techie sport and has spawned some incredibly advanced and impressive equipment—and with this comes the gearheads. What used to be just the cassette (basically) that was there primarily to hold your fly line has evolved into a piece of machinery rivaling the best-made bait-casting reels and coffee grinders. Don't get overwhelmed, though. I will walk you through the purchase of a new reel with these top ten things to look for in chronological order.

10: Capacity

It is commonly believed that you need a specific size fly reel for a certain weight or length of fly rod. But that is not true. Instead, think of the size of your reel more in terms of capacity. How much backing do you want on the reel? The average trout fisherman will go a lifetime without ever having a fish take enough off the reel to even begin to see the backing. However, if you are fishing larger rivers with larger trout, or not fishing for trout at all, then take the backing more seriously. And that raises another question: How heavy does the backing need to be? Almost every freshwater application requires 20-pound test, but do you need 30-pound? *Well . . . do ya, punk?* Remember, the heavier the backing, the less of it you can fit on any given reel. The weight of the actual fly line will take up different amounts of space as well. This is where the assumption about reel sizes matching rod sizes comes from, and it is why reel manufacturers usually specify the range in line sizes for a given model of reel.

9: Price Points

You can easily find fly reels in a wide range of prices. The low end of the spectrum is a plastic trout reel in the $35 to $45 range, and then the prices go all the way up to the big saltwater reel made of aircraft-grade aluminum anodized with sweet tarpon-scale graphics for, well, more than you ever need to spend on a solitary piece of fishing equipment. A good but reasonably priced fly reel will go from $120 to $300. The reels I covet the most run from $300 to $400, but my advice here is not black-and-white. Spend what you can afford on a reel; the appreciation of quality will always outlast the memory of a bargain.

8: Machined vs. Cast

If you are trying to get into this sport on a student's budget, don't fret too much about your reel. If you want something that you intend to use a lot and keep around for awhile, put down the plastics and even the nicer cast reels. These will eventually snap or crack and that is that. Find yourself a decent, machined-aluminum reel with as few plastic innards as possible. The bar stock that most quality fly reels start out as is very lightweight but tough. You may not think you need a super-tough reel on your 3-weight creek rod, but that is exactly the fishing situation where you need gear that will withstand constant abuse. You will be moving more frequently on these smaller trout streams, and often you will be doing an odd combination of rock climbing and redneck ballet. Your reel will take the brunt of this lifestyle choice.

Kevin Neiswander poses with a Mexican rooster. Saltwater reels need to have drags that can stop fish like this. RANDY HICKS

7: Warranty

When talking about fly rods, I will *always* recommend one with a lifetime breakage warranty. Fly reels are another story. All rods *will* break eventually—if they don't, you are not fishing enough. But I have owned some very inexpensive reels that have been severely abused and never slowed down or shown signs of wear (not counting the one million scratches). Most common breakages or problems that occur can easily be fixed for free or for a nominal fee at your nearest *competent* fly shop. The big plus side to this story is that all decent fly reels carry a lifetime warranty, and repairs will usually only cost you shipping.

6: Drag

Oh, what a drag. These may be my least comfortable conversations in the fly shop. It is not that it is a boring or long conversation, just that there is so much confusing and conflicting information out there on the Internet about reel drags . . . the new, the improved, the disk, the conical, the cork, the ultra-saltwater sealed. Read through a few sales brochures the fly reel reps have dropped off at any given fly shop, and you will leave feeling like the dumb kid in class, or under the false assumption that you are now a licensed aerospace engineer. My analysis is that other than weight—every company is attempting to make the first weightless fly reel—there is only drag system design left to one-up or compete with other reel companies. Most work *far better* than they will ever need to, the exception being big-game reels attached to the end of a 9- to 12-weight saltwater rod. In this case be sure the reel's drag is completely sealed to keep out water, sand, and salt. As far as the drag components themselves, I trust high-grade carbon because it will tolerate intense heat and will not wear out.

5: Arbor Size

Is this a large arbor reel? I get this question a lot, often when the reel is in the hands of the customer asking the question. The arbor is the center axis of the reel where the backing and fly line are wound onto. And it is difficult to find a reel without a large arbor. But there was a time when your standard arbor diameter was less than ¾ inch, and for most fly fishermen, times were just great. Then one reel manufacturer came out with a new reel with a slightly larger diameter arbor and really talked it up. It was all the rage. A guy could reel in his line in half the time! Then another company replied with yet another, newer reel with an arbor that dwarfed that of the last—the great arbor wars of the 1990s. *Good grief!* But all this silliness

that come with small clips, remove them and use parachute cord or old fly line as a replacement. The original clips *will* break eventually.

6: Versatile Fly Box

A lot has happened to fly boxes over the last few decades. Things were simple and choices were limited some years ago, but lately fly fishing has gotten more and more specialized and the fly selection has grown exponentially. A well-rounded angler has multiple specialized fly boxes these days, some with midges, some full of big attracter dry flies, and others stuffed with weighted streamers—and those are just the trout-specific boxes! The organizational juggling act happens when a fly fisher attempts to simplify the boxes and get the personal fly disaster in order. Having the right fly box (i.e., fly *boxes*) becomes paramount in successful fly organization—and everyone has the same, but very different, needs. I have found the Umpqua Pro Guide series of boxes to be the best designed for fishermen with specialized organizational needs and still offered at a good price.

5: Tippet Spool Tender

In a style of fishing that is as prone to knots and tangles as fly fishing is, but is so reliant on proper leader construction and rigging, it is no wonder fly shops sell so many pre-built leaders and spools of tippet. They sell *a lot*. Most beginning fly fishers carry maybe one or two spare 9-foot 5X leaders paired with spools of 5X and 6X tippet, and they keep them loose in one of their mainly empty vest pockets. *No problem.* But soon there will be a lot more junk collecting in those pockets and rerigging will start to get messy. Most trout fishermen carry a dozen or so different lengths and weights of tapered leaders and five spools of tippet minimum—as thick as 2X down to at least 6X. Leaders come in little plastic baggies, making them easy to store in a slim side pocket somewhere in a vest or pack, but once you have five to ten tippet spools

A good fly box is chosen in part based on the individual needs of the angler.

rattling around in the main compartment, things get in the way. Carrying your spools in an organized fashion on the outside of your pack is the best way to wrangle these cats. This also enables you to rerig faster on the water. I prefer simplicity in my tippet spool tender—something easy to load and unload, and doesn't add to the weight or bulk of my pack. Loon Outdoors makes a T-shaped tippet holder made from two short lengths of graphite tubing with a small attachment carabiner at the top.

4: Soft Cooler

There was a time (not so long ago) when I would be on the river before light and not stop or slow down until it was too dark at the end of the day to see a trout rise. I would never bring food, and rarely more than one small bottle of water. I would fish hard, through the rain or blistering heat, and collapse on my old futon at the end of the day with barely the energy left to microwave a three-day-old slice of pizza. I would become severely dehydrated and exhausted, and by the end of the day could hardly form a complete sentence. I probably caught a ton of fish—can't really remember. What I *do* remember is being hungry all the time. Now I eat breakfast and bring along a soft cooler with an ice pack, a jar of pickles, some cheese, and a sandwich. And an extra bottle of water. My fishing has gotten much more enjoyable, and I am able to fish better and complete most of my sentences.

3: Polarized Sunglasses

Spotting fish—or holding water and structure—is an acquired skill rivaling casting in one's ability to improve as a fly fisher. You can't sign up for a class that teaches trout spotting in order to improve your double haul, but there are three easy ways to spot more fish: *Spend more time on the water*—practice makes perfect sense, right? *Drink more water*—dry eyes are often mistaken as permanent vision

"Breakfast on a topo map . . . gonna be a good day!"

loss, especially in ultradry climates like what we have in Colorado. And *wear a good pair of polarized lenses*—the polarization eliminates the glare off the surface of the water and allows the angler a personal window underwater. Really, these are a must for any fly fisher.

2: A Good Map

Maybe the most valuable piece of equipment you can find in a fly shop is sold for $19.95: the big, bright red DeLorme Atlas & Gazetteer. This series contains some of the best and easiest-to-find maps you can buy. I have one for every state I have even *thought* about driving through. They have detailed topographic maps and show just about every back road and recreation site. The best features are the good fishing spots you add or highlight later with a stubby pencil or leaking ballpoint during road trips, or under the veiled secrecy of a fly shop.

1: Off/Mute Button on Cell Phone

The electronic leash can ruin a day of fishing faster than a canyon car wreck. Taking a cell phone on a river is like moving a television into the bedroom. You may still have a good time, *but not really.* The driving force behind the lives of serious fly fishers is the desire to be *away* from the office, the house . . . *life.* Don't bring the thing you are fleeing with you.

Chapter 6

The Top Ten Ways to Get What You Need at a Fly Shop

Somewhere along the way, fly shops got a reputation for being intimidating places where you are, more often than not, made to feel stupid, or at least receive a condescending attitude in response to your questions. I am sorry to say in some cases this reputation is not unfair. There are those in the fly-fishing industry who are emotionally used up, bitter, and generally too "salty" to be exposed to the general public. And there are fly shops that unintentionally breed this poor attitude. Usually it can be tracked back to a lousy owner. If you have a fly shop like this in your town, I hope you have another one close enough and good enough to warrant the drive. However, if you want to maximize the commodity of a local fly shop, here are some pointers that will improve your experience.

10: Do Some Homework

"I have never fished before, but this fly fishing looks pretty cool. What do I need to know?" If a guy wants to walk into a fly shop and say this, he can. Most shops are professional enough to steer this customer in the right direction and will probably be willing to give a forty-minute crash course free of charge. But don't *expect* this kind of service. Pick up a book about basic fly fishing and read it before you go into the fly shop. Or do some research online before asking a ton of questions. This will pre-educate you just enough to ask the right questions. You will always get better and more thorough answers if you ask three very direct questions vs. *three dozen* random questions.

9: Know Their Names

As a patron of a bar or a fly shop, you appreciate when the bartender remembers your choice of drink or when the guy at your local fly shop knows your name—and maybe even remembers what river you were headed to the last time you were in. Well, it works the other way around, too. And it helps the fly shop recognize you as a regular if you roll in and say, "Hey, Jay! How's business?" You say that, and I'll make you a priority for as long as you are in the shop. Another fine idea is sporting the fly shop logo, even if it's having a ball cap stashed behind the seat of your car that you don just before entering—*still* a great way to get what you need and probably a bit more. So walk in flying the right colors, and you will always get the hookup!

8: Help Me Help You

It's as simple as it sounds. If you come to me at the fly shop with a weird question or a vexing little problem, I *badly* want to help you out. But sometimes I just can't, because I have not been provided the right amounts of the right information. So if you have a fly question, bring in your fly box. If you have a rigging question, bring in your fly reel. If you have questions about fishing spots, bring in your gazetteer. If you have a hatch or bug question, don't ask about some black bug (or was it dark brown?) that was hatching on the creek about three weeks ago that may or may not have had tails. Every digital camera has a decent macro setting: Learn how to use it and catch that bug on the creek. This goes for flies as well. If you have a very specific fly in your box that is working exceptionally well one day and you are down to your last one, *take a photo of it!* Then you won't be the guy in the fly shop the next morning asking if I sell "a little brownish fly with some fluffy stuff on the top, about *this* big." Sure wish I could help!

7: Talk to Your Guide

The best fly-fishing guides have gigantic egos. This is an unarguable fact—some just hide it better than others. It's a good thing, though, and should work to your advantage as a client. Your guide wants the day to end with his client having caught more fish and learning more about fly fishing than ever before, and then with a big, fat tip to acknowledge the experience. Your guide wants you to have *the best day ever!* So this is sort of a guide-sport continuation of point number 8: Help your guide help you. Tell him exactly what you are hoping for, exactly how open to ideas you are, exactly what you *don't* want, and exactly why you hired him in the first place. And be honest about your skill level and experience before you get going. This information is valuable to your guide in choosing the best-suited venues and techniques to expose you to. And after the first cast, he will know *exactly* how badly you exaggerated.

6: Red Flags

Unfortunately, fly shop customers can do or say some things that will get them informationally blacklisted. This is usually for ethical reasons ("You guys sell any snaggin' hooks?") or a matter of professional survival. A fly shop will succeed as a business—or not—based on two hallmarks: education and satisfaction. This is why catch-and-release is preached like the gospel. I can't take you to the river and teach you how to fly fish if there are no fish. And I can't give you advice or sell you a new piece of equipment with the promise it will help catch you more fish, *if there are no fish!* So, as a general rule, if you ask about trout recipes or regulations (i.e., "What's the limit?"), do not, as a follow-up, ask to be let in on all the favorite fishing spots. Also, I feel I should mention that "Hey, I'm cleaning out my septic tank this weekend. Do you guys rent waders?" is never a good way to begin a productive customer-clerk relationship.

The free advice given at your local fly shop can bring you your best day of the season. ERIN BLOCK

5: Be Prepared to Get Information

If it is knowledge or tips you are seeking at a fly shop, be prepared to translate whatever you learn into something usable, or to do something about a hot lead. If you have the tendency to hold court or "dominate the rap, Jack" at your local shop, you likely have not learned anything there. Listen more than you talk. And always carry a good map in with you. When asked, a guide will rattle off five different places that are currently fishing well. He will talk fast and abbreviate important proper nouns. Have him stop and circle them on your map.

4: Common Courtesy

Don't be a tool. Don't even be *mildly* condescending to anyone working at a fly shop . . . if, of course, you want help or advice. No one cares if you are a big deal back on Wall Street, or king of your own cubicle island. Do not expect a warm reception and a ton of free information if you burst into any fly shop talking loudly in the general direction of nowhere because you're rocking a new earpiece phone and then approach a guide or shop guy with your sunglasses and earphone still stuck to your head ("Hey, buddy, where are all the hot spots? Hey, you work here?").

3: Don't Be a Vulture

Some of the best fly shops in the country are small, family-owned businesses. One of the owners is usually behind the register, and they may have one or two full-time employees and a handful of part-time shop guys/fly-fishing guides hanging around. These small shops survive in a world of e-commerce and big-box stores because the good ones have knowledgeable employees who are in the industry because they love what they do. But don't forget, these are still small businesses. They are rarely thriving enough to be as loose with their product and time as they project to the public. The bartender may smile and shake your hand and even be your friend, but he ain't going to give you a free drink and listen to a forty-minute rehash of your day when there are a dozen other patrons farther on down the bar. So don't be the one who makes the most cheerful guy in town start hating his job. Do your best not to be a time or attention vulture. And don't be the guy who mines a ton of product information from his favorite small fly shop and then rolls in a week later with a new reel, line, and backing (all sporting the very recognizable big-box bar code) and ask to get spooled up and ready to fish. Lastly, no matter where you are—in your local shop or on the road somewhere—*always* trade flies for information. Buy a half-dozen common dry flies or something else you know you can eventually use from the guy before you ask for the lowdown. That is proper fly shop etiquette.

2: Be Open to Suggestion

If you want to build a good relationship with your local fly shop and experience the best of the fishing opportunities you have available to you, you have to be open to suggestion. If you are dead set in your fishing habits, rivers, and fly choices, you are hurting only yourself. Learn and try out a new rigging technique, give some new shop-favorite flies a chance, put that napkin map to some remote lake in your pocket, or even try a new species of fish. Think about your fishing like a jam-of-the-month club: It makes a lousy Christmas bonus and you have no idea what is coming next, but it's jam, so how bad can it be?

1: Beer

I once had a customer bring me in a twelve-pack of beer because I had pointed him in the direction of a creek that was fishing particularly well. He had his father coming into town and needed somewhere close and easily accessible for an eighty-five-year-old equipped with cane fly rod and plastic hip . . . during runoff. But it worked out smashingly, and the guy was stoked that I gave up a secret spot because he was in a bind. And he showed his appreciation with a twelver. It was really cheap beer. I drank one after work and fed the rest to the feral fly-fishing guides loitering behind the shop. But that cheap box of aluminum cans bought that man a lifetime of hot flies and sweet new fishing spots.

Chapter 7

The Top Ten Ways to
Save Money in Fly Fishing

Initially, the most addictive element of fly fishing is the unpredictability of it all. You can head down to the same trout stream every day after work and never know for sure what is going to happen. I like to think of fishing success as riddles the bridge keeper asks. Sometimes it is as easy as "What is your favorite color?" But, brave Sir Robin, be prepared to know the capital of Assyria. If the riddle was always the same, few of us would last long in the sport. We would move on to other fun things, or maybe even something productive like splitting firewood or mowing the grass. But if it is this ever-changing degree of challenge that gets us *hooked* on fly fishing, it is the ability to take the sport and run as far as you want with it that can consume your life and your paycheck like a bad poker habit. So here are the ten best ways to leave the table with shirt intact.

10: Fish Local

Airfare is expensive. Gasoline is expensive. If you keep accurate records of what you spend every year to support your fly-fishing addiction, you may be surprised at how small of a percentage is spent on flies and gear. ExxonMobil and Frontier Airlines make out far better than Umpqua Feather Merchants and Sage Fly Rods. If you are looking for ways to trim the fat, the first thing to consider is spending more time fishing close to home.

9: Tie Your Own Flies

I hesitate to include fly tying in a list of ways to save money in fly fishing because, like family vacations and communism, it only works well *in theory*. It is true that you can purchase the hooks and materials to tie your own flies and it will save you a good bit of money. Eventually you will save yourself enough to consider all your initial investment paid off (such as the tying vise and tools). A large number of beginning fly tiers list monetary reasons as one of the main motivators to learn to tie. But in almost all cases it ends up the other way around—you will not be content keeping tying a chore and only tie what you need. It will turn into a hobby immediately, and before you know it, the spare bedroom turns into your designated tying area and you are spending more cash on materials than you ever did on flies—not to mention all the fancy new boxes you have to buy to house your rapidly expanding collection of every fly known to man and fish.

8: Build Leaders from Scratch

I do not build my own leaders from scratch, not anymore. But because I did for years, I never think twice about cutting into my existing leader, or adding to it whatever is needed to get done the job at hand. Too many beginning fly fishers spend an exorbitant amount of money on new leaders because they are not comfortable adding tippet material or rebuilding an older leader. I suggest buying six or eight spools of different-diameter leader material and forcing yourself to construct all your leaders for one season. Even if you do this for just the one year, the experience will forever give you the confidence to do things to your leader you may not have done otherwise. This not only saves you money, but will make you a better fisherman.

7: Dry Your Fly Boxes

Losing individual flies is a fact of life in fly fishing, but losing or destroying an entire box of good trout flies is a catastrophe. It's not uncommon to have a well-stocked box worth over $500 in flies collected over a period of years. And while there are a lot of waterproof boxes on the market these days, a rubber gasket works both ways. Once there is moisture inside the box—because you opened it in the rain or put away a wet fly—it is there until you open the box again and let it dry out. To keep moisture from saturating or ruining my flies, and to keep mold to a minimum, I habitually prop open my fly boxes on top of my refrigerator. This is a perfect short-term storage spot/drying rack because the motor on the back of the fridge is always warm and running. Also, it is out of reach of dogs, cats, and kids.

6: Take Care of Your Glasses

It does not take long in this sport to realize how important good polarized eyewear is to your overall enjoyment and success. Clear, correctly tinted optics are often the most critical piece of equipment on the water, because you can't cast to what you can't see. But the best lenses in the world are no good to anyone once they are scratched. Invest $12 in a set of Croakies to protect your $200 specs, or at least a soft lens bag to carry them in when not in use.

5: Take Care of Your Fly Line

You are easily going to pay $40 to $75 on fly line. When considering how much to invest, a good rule to keep in mind is that you should buy $1 worth of line for each day you're going to use it on the river. If you're spending that much, you want to take care of your investment. The act of casting is hard enough on a fly line, but I see anglers abuse their line more than any other part of their equipment. I think many fishermen take out pent-up frustrations on their unruly fly line. The line is inanimate; remember, *you* are the one who tied the knot. If you strip several feet of line off your reel for a long cast and it gets tangled up around some milkweed, don't yank at it until it's free. Walk back and untangle. And don't step on your fly line. What makes most modern lines float are millions of glass micro-balloons incorporated into the thick outside coating. If you step on your line too often, it will no longer float and you won't get your seventy-five days worth, and you'll be back in the fly shop complaining about how such-'n-such brand fly line stinks 'cause it sinks.

In the excitement of landing a big fish, don't snap your rod or tromp on your fly line. ERIN BLOCK

4: Take Care of Your Waders

John Gierach wrote a book (a compilation of select stories from six previous books, actually) titled *Death, Taxes, and Leaky Waders*. It is a clever name because these are all equally inevitable. Once you log your first day in a new pair of chest waders, the inevitable clock starts ticking. Then, once you notice that first cold spot on your leg, the wader life-support struggle begins . . . and won't end until the entire inside and half the outside is coated in ⅛ inch of Aquaseal. But still, there are measures that can be taken to fend off the end and squeeze as much life as you can from your existing waders. Always use gravel guards to keep the dirt and stones out from between your boots and the neoprene stocking feet of your waders. If you feel any gravel in your boot that has snuck past the guard, stop, take the boot off, and rinse it out. Be careful where you sit, too. And don't scoot around on your rear end. Hang your waders up out of direct sunlight in a safe, out-of-the-way spot once you're home. Don't leave them balled up and wet in the backseat of your car for the entire workweek.

3: Buy It to Turn It

This one takes some serious discipline, but will save you a packet if you have an iron will and some follow-through. Don't hoard fly-fishing equipment you are no longer using. Sell it for what you can and recycle those dollars into newer and presumably better gear. Granted, this works best on the bigger-ticket items like rods and reels, but if you take care of your stuff (and don't smoke), you can get pretty good returns on heavy rain jackets, gear bags, and vests and packs. If you think you have the self-control to pull this off, be sure to buy good equipment, as the good stuff holds its value better and is Craigslist friendly.

2: Pack a Lunch

This saves both time and money, and sometimes time on the water is even more valuable than money. Break out a small cooler and ice pack and make yourself a wrap or something. Or go with a couple Clif Bars and a full canteen. Either way, you will not need to leave the river to avoid starving or have to resort to gas station burritos or a greasy drive-through burger. But those are nickels and dimes—the packed lunch saves the most money on the evening drive home. It is much easier to drive past the expensive steak houses and bar-and-grills if you already have a little something in your stomach.

1: Organize

Have a designated place for all your late-season fishing gear. Good fold-over fingerless gloves are a must in the winter, and if you misplace them in early March, there's no way you will remember where to start looking come November. Organization saves money and frustration on all fronts. Be aware of what tippet and leader you are running low on so you aren't doubling up in a last-minute panic at the fly shop. Have your fly collection in order to avoid unnecessary purchases. The worst cash drain of all is unorganized or impulsive fly tying. Create a list of things you have run out of as you are sitting at your tying bench, and do your best to stick to the list once you are at the fly shop.

Chapter 8

The Top Ten Must-Know Knots and Rigging Techniques

Years ago, during my first season in the fly-fishing industry, I worked under a guy I'll call "Danny." I worked part-time in the fly shop, but also took any and all guide trips that were thrown my way. In addition, because I had proven I could show up on time and be a good guide, I was offered an assistant role in teaching the introductory fly-fishing classes. These classes were "taught" by Danny. Now, this guy was an incredibly intelligent person and a very good fisherman, but he wasn't a great instructor. I hung around and fetched whatever odds and ends he needed as class props and observed how *not* to teach fly fishing. Maybe the most important lesson I gained from that season was how not to unnecessarily overcomplicate the teaching of the important knots and rigging. Keep it simple, and only add to your repertoire once you are 100 percent fluent with the magic tricks you are currently practicing.

10: Reel and Line

Out of the gate I like to take the time to walk new fly fishers through the process of "lining up" their first fly reel. I don't, however, attempt to teach them how to tie an arbor knot, or even a nail knot for that matter. These are knots you will eventually teach yourself if you really get deeply involved in the sport, but it is almost pointless to take the time and temporarily sidetrack brain space for things you will inevitably forget in a matter of days. You will only retain those things

The sooner you become proficient at tying the basic knots and learn proper rigging, the sooner you will have good days on the water.

you do with some degree of repetition. I *do* want the beginner to see what I am doing in the reel-rigging process, though. This is an important first step in understanding the nuts and bolts of the sport and recognizing the differences between conventional gear fishing and this weird fly-casting thing.

As primitive as it all is, lining a fly reel is far more complicated than just winding 6-pound mono onto a new spinning reel. First there is the *backing,* which is usually 20-pound, white braided Dacron secured to the arbor of the reel. This backing serves several purposes, big-fish insurance being paramount. Most modern fly lines are only 90 feet, and a fish-of-a-lifetime could just turn into the current and take you much farther downriver—or "into the backing," as the phrase goes. The backing will help you out in other less glamorous ways, too, like filling up the reel and fattening the arbor diameter. This is important because the larger the diameter, the faster you can reel in the line, and it also cuts down on the coiling, pig-tailing, or "memory" that some fly lines and leaders will acquire if wound tightly around a small diameter for too long.

Once the backing is in place (usually between 80 and 200 yards depending on the size/capacity of the reel), I will then use a nail knot to attach this to the rear end of the *fly line* itself. I don't teach this nail knot on day one. It is hard to learn, impossible to retain, and way easier with the aid of a nail knot tool. Buy one of these tools and have someone at your local fly shop teach you next winter—or the winter after that. At the very terminal end of this thick, coated, and oddly colored fly line (the stuff you will actually be casting) is where the *leader* goes. Traditionally this is where you would tie another nail knot, but most good fly lines these days come with a loop built in at the end, allowing you the ease and luxury of doing a simple loop-to-loop connection from the end of the fly line to your leader, which is now offered pre-looped as well.

1.

2.

3.

4.

5.

6.

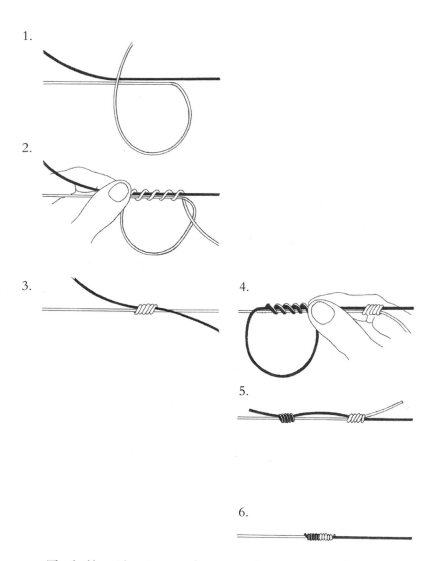

The double uni knot is strong, fast to tie, and can join many different materials.
KENDALL ZIMMERMAN

9: Leader to Tippet

The diagram I draw the most on the back of scrap paper at the fly shop is *not* one of half-secret backroads to get to the best stretch of the South Platte. It is a simple line drawing for customers who are confused about the difference between what is leader and what is tippet. Many first-year fly fishers assume these are two very different things, but they are not. The *tippet* is just one of the ingredients (the very terminal ingredient) of your leader. The *leader* is just the roughly 6 to 12 feet of nylon or fluorocarbon at the end of the 90 feet of fly line, the clear stuff you tie your flies onto and fish with. You can learn how to build your own leader (using a stack of progressively light leader material on spools), but most likely I am going to suggest you buy a standard, pre-looped packaged leader. These typically come in single or three-packs and in 7½-foot and 9-foot lengths. You *will,* however, need to know how to join two lengths of leader. Having a premade leader doesn't get you out of tying a knot. After enough snags and fly changes, breaking off 6 inches of leader here and biting off 3 inches there, you *will* need to lengthen your leaders. The most commonly used knots for this are the blood knot and the surgeon's knot, but I prefer a double uni knot. I began using this knot while building pike leaders and experimenting with different diameters of knottable wire and braided Spiderwire bite tippets. I have found it to be excellent for attaching two very different diameters or makes of leader material.

8: Tippet to Fly

This is the second of only two knots you *need* to know as a fly fisher. The most commonly used tippet-to-fly knots are the improved clinch and the Palomar. I use the former exclusively. It may not be the best knot ever used to lash on a fly or lure, but it is the one my dad took time out from his own fishing to teach me. And judging by the amount of time it took my mother to teach me how to tie my shoes, this must have been a very selfless and noble act on Dad's part. So if you already know a decent knot, something your dad showed you years ago, keep using it! If not, learn the improved clinch right now. No, no . . . don't keep reading. I mean go find a fly and a piece of string, line, or leader material *right now* and learn it! You want to fish, right?

Improved clinch knot. KENDALL ZIMMERMAN

Alrighty then . . . you're back. Good. Now let me complicate things just a bit. There is another tippet-to-fly knot I would like to mention, but keep in mind that this is not something you must know and practice—it's more one of those things you will have in the recesses of your mind to come back to a couple years into this new obsession of yours. The loop knot. Or drop loop knot. Or, because I usually use the improved clinch, the Rapala knot, which is very similar, just with one step added at the start. Any of these knots will suffice and serve the intended purpose, which is to increase the sink rate of a weighted nymph or the erratic action of a streamer. You can get away with using heavier leader/tippet material if you are using one of these loop-style knots because the line isn't cinched down on the eye of the hook, thus making the fly sink or move somewhat rigidly in the water.

7: Lake vs. River

The biggest concerns here are presentation and stealth. On small to midsize creeks and rivers, where you are likely to find fast water, braided water, or pocket water, you are going to usually want shorter, more compact leaders that allow you to make super-short, point-blank casts where you may only be casting the length of the leader and just enough fly line to add some casting weight out past the tip-top of the fly rod. A short leader will make those awkward, half-sidearm, half-do-whatever-it-takes casts much more doable in tight quarters. On lakes and/or wide, slow-moving stretches of river, your leader should normally be longer and wispier. When you are choosing a leader for one of these purposes, or building one with what you have, think about achieving the proper sink rate for deep lake fishing or achieving a long, drag-free drift for those long, slow glides on a large river or spring creek. The general idea with this type of leader is to put as much distance or slack between the end

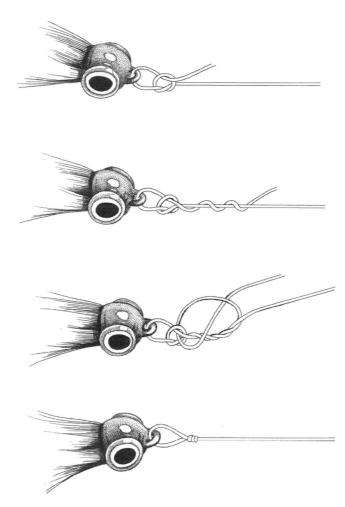

A Rapala knot is the best way to get good action from a big streamer fly.
KENDALL ZIMMERMAN

of the fat, obtrusive fly line and the fly. Start with a leader *at least* 9 feet long, and the only obstacles limiting maximum casting length are wind, the weight of your flies, and, of course, your casting ability.

6: Single Dry Fly

Dry fly fishing is not always the most productive way to catch a lot of trout, but it is unarguably the most fun. The single dry is the easiest, most straightforward rig in fly fishing. And everything is 100 percent visible—the drift, the rise of the trout, and the take. For these reasons it lends itself perfectly to beginning fly fishers. You can see where your cast ended up and see the current pulling on the leader and the fly (this is called *drag* and is bad, by the way), but you can see when you are doing everything correctly as well. You can see your fake fly on the water and compare it to the naturals, and you can see the fish eat, so there is no excuse not to set the hook.

5: Dry and Dropper

Once you are comfortable making the upstream cast and achieve the good, natural drift necessary to do well with the single dry fly, you are ready to double down and add a second fly to your rig. The dry and dropper is the most commonly used and most effective two-fly combination in stream fishing. The usual setup is a highly visible, super-buoyant dry fly . . . one that has a lot of foam or stacked elk hair to be able to carry the weight of the weighted nymph (or two) that you have hanging below. Then you have the weighted dropper—usually a bead-head nymph. The distance below the dry fly that you hang this nymph is determined mainly by the depth and speed of the water you are fishing, but as a rule, I rarely have it rigged shorter than 12 inches or longer than 24 inches. I will, however, often tie a second dropper nymph, making it a three-fly, dry-dropper-dropper rig. I attach the dropper flies using an appropriate-diameter spool of tippet material and the same knot used to tie the first fly on, only I am tying it to the bend of the hook.

4: Indicator Nymphing

Unfortunately, this is often the first taste of fly fishing many beginners get . . . if their first experience is a guided fly-fishing trip. Guides are *almost* always very good fishermen and *usually* at least decent teachers, but the majority of clients a guide has during a season tip based on quantity of trout caught, not knowledge gained or personal technique improved. So, you can't blame the guide for sticking you with a nymph and bobber—it is very effective and takes almost no thought, minimal casting, and only a small amount of skill in line control. In essence, it is the guide's malpractice insurance. The general idea with an indicator nymph rig is some sort of easy-to-lob-upstream bobber that is able to suspend one to three weighted nymphs on the drift back downstream and quite possibly a heavy piece of lead split-shot to boot. Commonly the fly is tied on first, and then the split-shot is pinched onto the leader 6 to 12 inches above the fly. The indicator (or bobber) is tied or looped onto the leader well above that, usually at least a few feet. The amount of split-shot you use, as well as the distance the shot is from the fly and the distance up the leader you want to place the indicator, will be determined by how deep the water is, how fast the water is moving, and, of course, where the trout are holding in all this. A good rule to remember when indicator nymphing is to adjust the weight and depth of your rig multiple times before even considering changing your flies. All the trout would like to eat your flies—they probably just haven't seen them yet!

3: High-Stick Nymphing

This form of nymph fishing has almost the identical rigging as the indicator style mentioned above, minus one key ingredient—the bobber. Often referred to as tight-line nymphing or eastern nymphing, this is a deadly deepwater and pocket water strategy. It does take more touch, talent, and concentration than watching a bright orange bobber float downstream, however. It is rigged with one or two nymphs and a split-shot or two above that, same as before, but you must keep the rod tip high and out over as much of the current as you can. The entire line, leader, and tippet that is out past the tip of the fly rod needs to be as taut as possible so you can feel the split-shot bounce on the boulders below and the often subtle hesitation you feel when a trout eats. When practiced correctly, this method will take more fish because your fly is following the irregular contours of the stream bottom, not a static line controlled by a bobber.

2: Euro-Nymphing

Czech nymphing, French nymphing, Spanish nymphing . . . they all have their similarities and idiosyncrasies. And the entire Euro-nymphing craze that hit the United States fairly recently is both awesome and annoying all in the same day. This is a very technical and incredibly effective form of fly fishing born of European fishing competitions. These fly-fishing competitions, as well as their traditions and styles, have crossed the pond and infiltrated the culture of American fly fishing. This is the awesome part: It adds greatly to the arsenal of knowledge and information at our disposal. The basic gist of this form of nymphing is the same as high-sticking, but minus the lead split-shot. In these competitions there are many strict rules about how you can rig your flies. The flies must all be barbless (hence the influx of newly designed "competition hooks" that come with extra-long spears to aid in holding fish), there can be no weights or lead attached to your line or leader, and bobbers or strike indicators are *strictly verboten!* This forces the fisherman to be very careful with the rig setup and the weight distribution of the nymphs involved. Some of the nymphs tied for this style of fishing are incredibly heavy—known as "anchor" nymphs to get the multi-fly rig down deep without the luxury of split-shot. Again, it is an amazingly effective form of fly fishing, and many of the modern advancements that we all take for granted (such as bead-head nymphs and better barbless hooks) come from this competition fishing. The annoying aspect of this style invasion is the *mystique* so many American fishermen have bathed the whole thing in. It is not some secret form of Peruvian fly rod jujitsu practiced by gray-bearded masters in ancient, faraway mountaintop ruins . . . It is just high-sticking with a couple of gear limitations.

1: Streamer and Wet Fly Fishing

I have included these together as the final part of this section for several reasons, but primarily because the same basic rigging, casting, and fishing techniques are used for both—and the flies themselves are fairly interchangeable, too. Generally, any fly that imitates a young fish, sculpin, crayfish, or leech is considered a *streamer*. The term *wet fly* is, on one hand, simpler and yet also semantically more complicated. There was a time (a simpler time) when there were only two classifications of flies: the dry fly and the wet fly. The immature life stages of aquatic insects were imitated by flies fished below the surface, known as *wet flies*. The grown-up, or adult, life stages of these same insects were fished on the surface of the water, mimicking the way the actual bugs hatch on the surface or come back to the surface to lay their eggs; these were called *dry flies*. Nowadays we have gotten all anatomically correct and species specific and life-cycle nuanced— you know, *overcomplicated*. We now have fly shop bins full of nymphs, pupae, larvae, emergers, duns, cripples, stillborns, and spinners, oh my! Yet, there remains a classification of subsurface fly called a *wet fly*. They are not found in every fly shop and they don't look like any

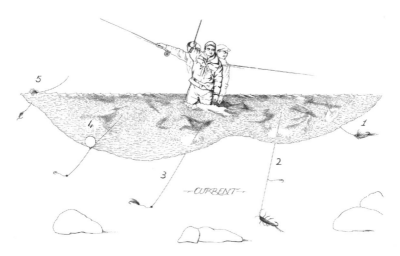

Kendall Zimmerman

one particular species of Latin-sounding fly fisherman's bug, but they work just as well now as they did way back when . . .

The proper way to rig and fish either a streamer or a wet fly is on an average-length to slightly-shorter-than-average-length leader. It is also wise to use a much stronger tippet on big streamers because they can draw incredibly vicious strikes that can easily snap a lighter leader. You will then do everything exactly opposite of what you have learned to do with a dry fly or a nymph. You will move and cast downstream instead of up, you will drop your rod tip almost into the water instead of reaching out and up as far as you can, and you will give the fly as much against-the-current action as you can—a frantic, erratic, crippled, and scared action, actually. And be prepared to meet some of the bigger, meaner, and more aggressive fish in the river.

Chapter 9

The Top Ten Ways to Improve Your Fishing

The underlying goal of every fly-fishing "how-to" ever written is to help you, the reader, become a better angler. Also, the main motivator for struggling or aspiring fly fishers to take a class, hire a guide, or ask questions at their local fly shop is to gather the knowledge that will lead them into more and better fish. My job, as the author of this book and as the warm body in a fly shop, is to offer up the advice. And I wish I had the secret fly I could hand everyone looking for a leg up—a fly that will be guaranteed to solve all casting issues, grant the recipient more time on the water, and never be susceptible to snags. But I do not. There are, however, subtle things you can do that will begin to enrich your experience on the water and improve your fishing. Here are the top ten ways to achieve this.

10: Get in Shape

Done well, fly fishing takes a degree of athleticism. You are rarely standing still for long, always moving from place to place, pool to pool, over all sorts of boulders and logjams. Sometimes fly fishing looks like an overdressed homeless man attempting to do a ballet through an abandoned army obstacle course. So get in shape—you will *perform* better.

9: Learn to Tie

If you get set up to tie all your own flies, you *may* save some money, but you will certainly end up with twenty times the fly arsenal. The quantity of fly choices itself is not the reason your fishing will improve; it is the chances you will take and places you will be more likely to cast into knowing you can easily afford to lose some flies. You will no longer feel the need to wade out and spook a pool to retrieve a three-nymph rig. You will snap it off and attempt to get your flies back after the pool is fished—maybe. Tying your own can give you an even better edge if you are willing to divert from the original, store-bought flies you started with and slowly convert them into custom-tweaked patterns perfectly engineered for the palates of your local trout.

8: The Long Rod

Like a good sniper rifle and Bell Telephone, a longer fly rod gives you the ability to reach out and touch someone. Good presentation and proper drift are almost always more important than fly or tippet choice—so anything that aids your ability to reach over currents or mend line is worthwhile. Do not be afraid of 4- and 5-weight rods well over 9 feet long, even on small, brushy creeks. When I was sixteen years old, I got laughed out of a fly shop in Pennsylvania for asking to see a 10-foot 5-weight—now these rods are showing up everywhere.

7: Partner Up

Fish with people who have more energy and talent than you. Never pass on an opportunity to fish with someone you know is an accomplished fly fisher. You can pick up so many good habits and new tricks this way—things you never would have thought to ask. If you go into the day with an open mind and are observant, you will always improve your game. If you are the best angler in your group of friends, then consider hiring a guide from a reputable local outfitter. Most outfitters are first-rate and have guides who know more about fly fishing than your eight-year-old nephew knows about the Pleistocene.

6: Document the Day

The most accurate source of local fishing information will always be your own journal. For the first year of recording, it may be worthless; however, every year *after the first* it becomes exponentially more valuable. You might remember an epic trip to the Green River two years ago when you hooked a hundred trout on #18 Blue-Winged Olive dry flies and you want to plan a return trip . . . but was it in April? Or maybe it was May? Use your camera as well. Take scenic shots of the river every time you go, then date the photo and record the water flow (cubic feet per second). Switch over to macro and take shots of the flies that are working that day and any of the natural insects you can capture in midair or under rocks. These fly and bug photos are a huge advantage when you walk into a fly shop asking for something specific. Getting online and starting a blog to journal your fishing is a great way to easily store the digital photos of the river and flies, as well as a brief description of the day. Several blog platforms are available to choose from, and most are free. And remember, there are privacy settings if you don't want to share your fishing life with some stranger in Australia—but *that can be fun, too!*

5: Attention to Detail

Often the difference between an average day on the river and the most epic day of the season comes down to some very small but crucial details. Pay attention to these small things to give yourself a fighting chance to land the big fish of the trip or make the cast necessary to put your fly in the right spot. Check for knots and nicks in your leader. Stretch your fly line and wind it back on your reel evenly to avoid unnecessary drama once a big fish is hooked. Inspect your rig after every few casts and remove the small amounts of moss or unidentifiable gunk that will inevitably gather on your flies. Check the sharpness of your streamer hooks. Rerig. Get those flies in front of the fish. Mend. Recast . . .

4: Cross Train

No matter how long you work at something, you will not reach your full potential if you restrict your interests. I once knew an amazing scientist who was confused by the functions of a soda vending machine. On the other hand, football players in the NFL take dance classes to improve their agility. *Imagine 300 pounds of agile!* I have a large number of customers who spend all year drifting nymphs with a 4-weight and then treat themselves to ten days of saltwater fly fishing. The first nine days are filled with blown shots at permit, trout sets on tarpon, and a sunburned guide who has gone hoarse from yelling. If this sounds painfully familiar, find your nearest mudflat and embrace the common carp. It will greatly improve your fish-spotting abilities, your long-range accuracy, and your stripping hook-sets. You will become the hero of the Bahamas next time you go—I promise. If you like to break out your heavy rod in the fall and swing big streamers to brown trout but it takes you awhile to adjust, consider bass or pike fishing a few times throughout the spring and summer. Who knows? You might get hooked on that, too.

3: Fish Harder

How do you improve your 2-mile time? *Run faster.* The same father/drill sergeant philosophy works with fishing, too. *Fish harder.* Don't dally with your gear. String up and get moving. Walk farther. Cover more water. Fish more. Keep your flies in the water more. Don't fuss with snags and messy tangles. Cut it off and build a new

Fish places others don't bother to. Eva Zimmerman holds up a largemouth bass caught in a neglected local farm pond.

rig—fast! *Let's go!* Never become complacent. If you are there to fish, don't lollygag.

2: Fish Smarter

The *fish harder* mentality works better for those who are younger and more energetic. Persistence, stubbornness, and determination will gain you many fish, but never as many as experience. However, it is all these younger, exuberant things that are needed as the building blocks. My favorite quote of all time is almost 800 years old: "Good judgment comes from experience. Experience comes from bad judgment." Right? So fish smarter. Pay attention to what the fish and the bugs are doing. Be aware of other anglers. Keep your dry flies floating. Nymph deeper. Adjust everything else before you blame a lack of fish on your fly choice. Let the weather and the season dictate how and what you do. And remember, a poor day of fishing is the one you learned nothing from, regardless of how many fish you landed.

1: Fish Places Others Don't

There is a difference between improving as a fisherman and improving your fishing. Spending time on technical, heavily pressured tailwaters can sharpen your skills finer than any other whetstone. However, the best way to improve your fishing is to fish places others don't. Hike farther and higher than the will of other anglers. Bypass the easy-to-access pools and tempting stretches of stream within sight of the road—keep going farther. Fish the gnarly places and shallow riffles others avoid or walk past without thought, because these are often places the best fish live.

Chapter 10

The Top Ten Tricks of the Trade

Fly fishing is not a sport you easily master—it is too complex and unpredictable. But as long as you spend time on the water, you will never stop learning and improving. Your casting will come easier, you will spot and hook more fish, and you will land bigger ones. Before long friends will want you to teach them, and you will be the fly-fishing go-to at all the office parties. Semi-strangers will ask you painful questions during those awkward social situations when conversation is mandatory. *So you fly fish. What's that like?* That's fine, you would love nothing more than to hold court and tell all you know about this newfound passion of yours—but you only know enough after the first season or two to be self-sufficient. There are some things that take many more years to figure out. Here are my own ten best *hard-earned* lessons.

10: The Tuber Hatch

The tuber (*Sloppyahoo coloridae*) is one of the largest and most prolific aquatic insect emergences in the Rocky Mountain West. The "season of the tuber" usually begins in July (great Fourth of July hatch), reminiscent of the Mother's Day caddis on the Arkansas or the Yellowstone and lasts well through the end of August. The hatch often tapers down to almost nothing once the kids head back to school. The best time to catch the tuber hatch is on the hottest, sunniest days. This happens to be the polar opposite of the blue-winged olive mayfly hatch that prefers overcast, rainy days. Midday and early afternoon are the best times to find adult tubers on the water. *And they are never a welcome sight!* They can seriously disrupt your fishing. As a fly fisher you have three options: (1) You can drive farther up the river to faster, colder water where there are no tubers. (2) You can drive farther downriver, past diversion canals, where the stream flow may be too low to attract the tubers. (3) You can stay put and try to catch a few trout between flocks of scantily clad college students. This option is sometimes fun if you enjoy being the judge of your own private swimsuit contest. But you can still catch fish. Stand in the middle of the creek and observe the next "flotilla" as it makes its way down the creek or river toward you. Watch closely and take note of the route the tubers are taking. Step aside, let all the tubers pass you by, then move upstream and cast to all the side pockets that they haven't disturbed. You may be surprised by the luck you have!

9: Dealing with Ducks

Often while fishing near town (especially during winter) you will have to deal with tame ducks. They become trained by people tossing bread out for them. This causes a serious problem, because the ducks will see you fishing and assume the dry fly or indicator you are casting is a little treat intended for them, and will race each other to get at it. You can wave your arms and shoo them off, but not before they put down all the trout in the pool you are fishing. Also, if you do scare them off, the entire flock will likely fly off the water and crash back down in the next good pool upstream. This can go on all day and completely spoil the fishing. One good trick is to get out of the water and sneak around them, getting just upstream enough from the flock to push them all back downstream where you have already fished. If you are fishing with a partner, you can get the flock's attention by throwing out snow or dead leaves. Once you have all the ducks heading in your direction, your partner can easily get upstream.

8: Dealing with Other Anglers

Most random anglers pose no threat to your own fishing. If you do stumble onto another fly fisher who seems fairly competent, there are maneuvers you can make to ensure good fishing for yourself and still adhere to proper stream etiquette. If the other fisherman is moving upstream and you want to get in ahead of him, you should always leave a couple hundred yards of stream between you, or at least a handful of pools. The problem arises when that other fisherman knows you are up ahead and decides to leapfrog *you* upstream. Preventing this is simple—don't let the other guy know you're there! Sneak around and go into the creek just up and out of sight, and fish hard and fast so the other guy never gets close enough to see you. If you suspect you are on the receiving end of this bit of underhandedness, there are countermeasures. First, you must be aware of what is going on. If you are moving upstream and catching a trout or two in every likely pool and pocket, then for no apparent reason you blank on several good spots in a row, *red flag!* Look around for fresh boot prints in the mud or water splashed up on rocks. If you notice these things—or still seriously suspect someone is up ahead of you—get out of the creek and walk briskly upstream to try to locate the problem. Often you will do this and never find anyone ahead of you. This can mean there was someone fishing that stretch of creek earlier in the day and has since left. That's all right—just keep popping down to fish random pools until you find one that fishes like it hasn't been meddled with yet, and resume your serious fishing from that point on.

7: Fishing with a Partner

Always remember, two is fun, three is a crowd. There are four ways to work a small stream with a partner:

1. "Leapfrog" is the maneuver most commonly used. The two fishermen move upstream (or downstream if they are fishing streamers) and alternate pools. If the lead fisherman jumps ahead more than one run or pool, make sure to watch where he reentered the stream so you don't fish the same water.

2. "Sides" is just as it sounds—one fisherman on either side. This is more often used on larger streams but can be done on small creeks if one or both of the fishermen are experienced casters. If one of the fishermen is right-handed and the other is a lefty, things will work out even better.

3. "Clean up" is two fishermen moving up or down the creek on the same side, but not leapfrogging. The lead fisherman moves up- or downstream and the clean-up guy follows and tries to hit the pockets the other has missed or not covered thoroughly. This strategy is best used if one of the fishermen is a guest or he is less experienced and you want him to have the best possible opportunity to catch fish by having all the virgin water. If you find yourself in the clean-up position, you can try two different approaches: You can watch the lead fisherman closely and cast to the missed and hard-to-reach pockets, or you can use a vastly different rig. If the leader is casting a #16 dry and #18 nymph as a dropper, you can nymph with a couple #20 midge pupae deep with split-shot or go big with a stonefly the size of a double A battery.

4. "Switch" fishing is when both fishermen stay together and take turns taking the lead and casting. Pick something—one landed trout, three missed trout, or whatever—then switch positions. This is a load of fun, but in order for it to work out well, the two fishermen have to be close friends and longtime fishing partners.

Tim Drummond is a professional fly-fishing guide—for him, a spooked trout means no paycheck. TIM DRUMMOND

6: The Things That Scare Fish

There are many things that will spook fish. Most of their threats come from above the surface of the water—raccoons, herons, and, *of course,* fishermen. With this in mind, here is a list of things to be wary of:

- *Bright clothing.* Wear a drab-colored shirt and hat. While you are getting dressed, try to think about the environment. If you will be on a high-elevation stream surrounded by spruce and deadfall, woodlands camouflage is ideal but olive drab is just fine. If you are going to be in a canyon, think about wearing light khaki to blend in with the dry ground and boulders.

- *Shadow.* In the early morning and late afternoon, be very conscious of your shadow. Try to keep it off the water. Plan your route upstream, and where you stand to cast, with your shadow in mind.

- *Silhouette.* This is often overlooked but can be as detrimental as your shadow. Be careful how you approach the water, especially in a canyon when you park along the road and scramble down to begin fishing. Always be aware of the landscape behind you. Objects in motion can be spotted very easily if the only backdrop is bright blue sky.

- *Noise.* You can shout, scream, and squeal as loud as you like if you see a big trout. It won't hear you. The sound of your voice will bounce off of the surface of the water. What the fish *will* hear is the slightest ground vibration, so be careful wading or walking. Heavy footfalls, rocks being dislodged, gravel or studded boots grinding underfoot—all sound like big trouble to small-stream trout. A good exercise for all anglers is the bathtub test: Fill the tub, slide into the water so your head is completely submerged, and then have a "significant other" tell you an animated story. Can you hear this person? Nope. Now gently scratch the bottom of the bathtub. *Loud,* yeah?

Take all these things into consideration and note how close you get before a fish spooks, then create an imaginary halo around you at that distance. Make all your casts at that distance or greater. It's a simple strategy—let the trout see your fly before it sees you.

5: Setting the Hook

When a trout takes your fly on a small stream, you have to be careful how you set the hook. The two most common errors are setting the hook too hard (known as the *kung fu hook-set*) and setting the hook straight up. The problem with setting the hook too hard is twofold: You can easily break light tippet material on larger fish, or you can tear the fly out of the mouth of smaller fish. The problem with setting the hook straight up is noticed only if you miss the strike and find your fly hung in the tree branches 12 feet over your head. Set the hook horizontally and downstream. This way you are hooking the trout by pulling the hook into the corner of its mouth and, if you miss the fish, you will be making a downstream backcast instead of getting a snag. If you are fishing a larger dry fly and have a trout come up and eat, wait a split second before setting the hook. This allows the trout to close its mouth around your fly, turn down, and only then get the hook pulled into the corner of its mouth. It is admittedly difficult to do absolutely nothing for that split second, however, so train yourself to immediately drop your rod tip almost into the water (from the high-stick position) when the fish takes, and then give the downstream hook-set.

4: Nymphers Do It Deeper

Trout live at the very bottom of a trout stream. The bottom is where it is the safest, where most of the food is, and where the least current is. So, if there is no hatch, no rising or suspended feeding fish, you have to try to get a nymph down deep and hopefully in front of a trout. And more often than not, fly fishers don't get their flies down deep enough. If you are not hanging up on the bottom or losing flies, you are not nymphing deep enough. Use weighted nymphs and add split-shot to your leader before taking the time to second-guess your fly choice. And look for an excuse to set the hook on every drift—it may just be the fly or the split-shot bouncing on the bottom, but you aren't out anything if you set the hook anyway.

3: Become a Thief

Always on the run like Jesse James, you should cover lots of water as you go, picking pockets and robbing banks. Never pass up those small, one-trout pockets of water behind boulders that take an extra minute to maneuver over to. Many other fly fishers will not put in the work necessary to find all the fish in a given stretch of river. Get in there and do the work. Pick all the pockets on the subway . . . Even get the bum asleep on the bench. And get those flies in tight to the bank—especially when you are casting from a drift boat. Try to make the fly touch dirt at the start of every drift. You may lose more flies, but I guarantee you will catch more fish.

2: Locked and Loaded

Always be prepared to cast. Have your leader cleared past the rod tip, with enough line loose in your non-casting hand and the fly held at the ready—locked and loaded and the safety off. If your weapon jams (line tangles), take a knee and—with haste—rectify the situation. But don't get too stubborn on the wicked bad tangles. Cut it off and redo the entire rig if it will be faster. Get up and back in the game.

1: One Shot, One Kill

Make that first cast count. Even the dumbest stocked trout will spook if the presentation or the pickup is sloppy. And the big fish of the trip will only eat once . . . if you're lucky. So be sure the memory coils are stretched out of your leader, there are no nicks or accidental knots in your tippet, and you have complete confidence in your choice of flies and rigging. Remember, the likelihood of hooking a fish drops exponentially with each consecutive cast into a pool.

Chapter 11

The Top Ten Rules of Etiquette

We have all heard the term *stream etiquette* at some point or another. It is a deep-seated part of the sport-fishing culture. The origins of sport fishing and hunting are drenched in moral concepts such as fair chase and respect for your fellow man. Boiled down, it ends up as a healthy mix of Abrahamic values and a Native American relationship with the natural world. But time passes and things change, technology evolves and the population grows, and these ethics and rules of etiquette have been diluted or forgotten. But I refuse to stop carrying the torch—even if I suspect the coliseum at the end of the run has been torn down and replaced by an auto dealership.

10: Show Up on Time

Never be late for a fishing trip. No one cares if you were at the bar until 2 a.m. and show up red-eyed and then pass out on the stream bank until noon . . . as long as you're at the meeting spot five minutes before you said you would be. We have all watched the iconic "Buster wants to fish" scene from *A River Runs Through It*. It is an iconic scene for a reason.

9: Hot Spotting

Fly-fishing writers walk a thin line between giving good advice, getting people jazzed up to fish, and hot spotting places that can't handle the fishing pressure that follows. Crossing that line is a cheap way to get published and is *never* cool. I once hiked to a remote lake in the high country with friends and had three incredible days of catching greenback cutthroats on dry flies. The trout were plentiful and gullible, and they were larger than what is commonly found in the area. I had packed in a small video camera and collected some footage that, after hours of editing, turned into a fun "fly-fishing short" on YouTube. One of the reasons the editing was so tedious was that I was careful to trim any bits that mentioned the name of the lake or that panned up to reveal too much and give away the exact location. There are thousands of lakes in the Colorado high country that have incredible fishing, but a video pinpointing one would draw an incredible amount of fishing pressure to that particular lake. So I was careful. A year later a six-page article with full-page color photos came out in one of the major fly-fishing magazines mentioning the lake by name and blowing this remote, pristine jewel completely out of the water. Apparently a group of guys saw my movie online and became determined to fish that exact lake. It took them many months of research and snooping, but they figured it out. And they, too, had an incredible few days of fishing. *Awesome!* Then they wrote the article. Now every day in the summer multiple fishermen hike up there, leave over-fought trout floating belly up, and scatter trash on the banks. It cost me a valued friendship with the guy who shared that secret with me.

8: Boat Culture

Many fishermen in landlocked regions (such as the Rocky Mountain West) have never been exposed to maritime etiquette—and some of these guys even own their own drift boat. So, here are some general rules to abide by when you are a guest on someone's boat: *Always* ask the skipper for permission to board. *Never* wear studded wading boots in a drift boat or black-soled shoes on a saltwater flats boat. (Studs tear up boat hulls and black rubber soles leave scuff marks on white decks.) And *under no circumstances* pack a banana in your lunch.

7: Catch-and-Release

If we all killed two trout for dinner (half a legal limit in many places) on our home creeks every time we fished them, there would be no wild fish left. Then the state would be compelled to use tax dollars to stock the creek with hothouse rainbows (pale, weak versions of the real thing), and few serious anglers would be interested in the creek anymore and beginning fly fishers would lose interest in the sport altogether. Fly shops would then go out of business. This is my livelihood and *playing with my money is like playing with my emotions, Smokey!* I understand the weird hypocrisy of letting all your trout go, only to stop at the grocery store on the way home to buy fish or some other meat for dinner. I get it and I appreciate it, but wild trout and bass and pike are far too precious to be merely harvested. I also make a living teaching others about the satisfaction that comes with learning something like fly fishing, and I need *real* fish in the streams to accomplish this. If you must keep a mess of fish from time to time, be careful what species you take and from where you take them. Do your meat hunting in places that can benefit from culling, like a perch and crappie lake, or some remote beaver pond with stunted brookies.

6: Exaggerated Reporting

Fishermen lie, or at least we have the reputation for severe exaggeration. I'm bored with this trite attempt at a truism. If you have a habit of fabricating fish tales or adding extra pounds or inches, I hate to break it to you, but your fishing buddies are already onto you and probably have running jokes about it behind your back. It's common to have to "calibrate" reports from certain fishermen we know to be yarn spinners. *Don't be this joker!* Anyone who has fished for any length of time can smell fresh BS from a mile down the trail. On the flip side, there is no enamoring trait in a fisherman larger than a willingness to admit to a skunking, or a lost fish, or a fall in the river.

5: Barbless Hooks

Assuming you are practicing catch-and-release and not out there decimating the wild trout population, you ought to be pinching down your barbs. Barbs are meant to hold the hook point deep in a fish's jaw, so even if you are careful, you will do unnecessary damage to the fish when you remove the fly. Many first-year fly fishermen claim to crimp their barbs but actually don't, because they have not landed enough trout yet to be at peace with losing one now and again. Beginners also take awhile to figure out how detrimental slack line is when fighting a fish, and a barb makes up for this lack of skill. Once budding anglers have graduated out of their "white belt," they will begin to appreciate the advantages of a barbless hook. They're safer and easier to remove from a trout, your net, your shirt sleeve, and your ear. It takes only one time getting a barbed fly buried deep into your own body to make you swear to crimp *everything* from then on.

4: Redd Raiding

In the world and culture of fly fishing, it has *never* been considered kosher, fair chase, or sporting to catch or snag a female fish off her redd. *Never.* It does not matter if the brown trout in a particular drainage can't spawn successfully anyway, or if it's the largemouth bass of a lifetime on a nest right by the boat dock. *Never.* Redd raiding is unsporting at its best and severally damaging to the future of a fishery at its worst. The female fish is already under a great deal of stress as it is; hooking and landing her is often enough to force a complete and random egg discharge; and in the case of a big female bass, it allows other species—such as bluegill—to move in quickly and devour all the eggs already in the redd.

3: Give Others Space

Be respectful of other anglers. Fly fishing is only a social sport back at camp, or in a fly shop or within a small group of fishing buddies. If you run across a lone fly fisher on a trout stream or a couple working down the shoreline, they are likely enjoying the solitude and excited about the fishing prospects ahead of them. *Don't ruin their day!* Don't dare be a "high holer" by jumping directly in front of someone on a stream. The fisherman moving upstream has the right-of-way and a fisherman moving downstream must yield to him. Regardless of the situation, do your best to stay completely out of sight. If you accidentally stumble upon another fisherman and have gotten too close before seeing him, do everything possible to detour or backtrack softly, taking every precaution not to spook any fish. Give an apologetic wave and nod much like the one you give the fellow motorist you just accidentally cut off in traffic.

2: Be a Steward

Pick up after yourself as well as those who came before you. Leave the river (and the rest of the world, for that matter) better than how you found it, or were birthed into it. Put your cigarette butts in a plastic bag in a vest pocket, and shove your used leaders down the front of your waders. And save room somewhere to pack out at least two old, sun-faded cans of Tecate.

1: Respect the Fish

The entire sport revolves around these magnificent fish we pursue. There would be no rod makers or fly tiers or river keepers, and certainly no fly-fishing writers, if it were not for the fish. Don't disrespect the things that bring us so much pleasure and fulfillment. There is a shortage of such things in this life, so don't cheapen the rare treasures we do have. Don't set out to "rip some lips" or "stick a

Always wet your hands before handling trout. ERIN BLOCK

few"—these are tired ways of cheapening a noble sport. Above all else, be careful handling fish. Always wet your hands so as not to remove the fish's protective slime. Don't keep the fish out of the water for too long, and never hold one out over dry land or the hard bottom of a boat—it will inevitably squirm from your grasp and damage itself. Do your best to remove your fly from the fish as fast as possible, which is much easier if your barbs are crimped. Even a barbless hook will sometimes lodge into a hard piece of cartilage or deep down near the gills. When this happens, try twice and then give the fish your fly. You may need to buy or tie more flies this way, but the hooks will rust out quickly and most of the fish will survive. The idea is to do as little damage as possible and get the fish back into the water as quickly as you can. Don't be too caught up in the glory of the moment and accidentally kill the fish because you wanted just the right photo. And resist sticking a stomach pump down the fish's gullet. Using a stomach pump is like peeking at an opponent's cards in a poker game and then patting yourself on the back when you call his bluff. Respect those you love—don't cheat them.

Chapter 12

The Top Ten Ways to Improve Your Casting

The fundamental difference between casting a fly and casting conventional tackle is the weight of the lure. A spinning rod or bait caster is used to launch the weight of the lure or bait rig, while a fly rod is used to cast the weight of the line itself—this is because the common trout fly weighs, well, about nothing. With proper instruction anyone can learn a fishable fly cast in about ten minutes. Many of the fish-producing casts on a trout stream are less than 30 feet away, and the length of a fly rod takes almost a third of that distance away before the cast even begins. Besides, as my friend Kirk Deeter once wrote,

There is no such thing as the perfect cast. There are only casts that catch fish and casts that do not. CORINNE DOCTOR, REPYOURWATER.COM

"There is no such thing as the perfect cast. There are only casts that catch fish and casts that do not." With that said, here are the ten most common reasons for fishless casts and how to fix them.

10: It's All in the Wrist

Sure . . . as in all your casting problems are probably because you are trying to use your wrist. If you are holding a light, 9-foot fly rod and are attempting to put a single, small dry fly back at the head of a run 15 feet away, then using nothing but your wrist won't cause any problem at all. But once you need to put a little power behind a cast, you need to incorporate more powerful parts of your body. Keep your wrist rigid and use your forearm, shoulder, and sometimes even your waist and legs. Good distance casters, like good boxers, understand where their power comes from.

9: Lack of Authority

There are few things more painful for a fly-fishing guide than to watch a large rainbow eagerly sipping bugs from the surface of a lake, and having a client who casts like a politician attempting to explain a tax return. An authoritative but ultimately badly timed cast *probably* will end in failure, but a meek attempt to put a fly out any significant distance will *never* work. Often a poor caster will have a very good forward stroke (casting being the combination of two distinct arm motions) but have a weak, tentative backcast. This poor backcast sets up the forward cast for complete failure. Make your casting strokes like you mean it, keep them moving in a straight line, and end them abruptly. Let me say that last part again. *End your casting strokes abruptly!* Like you are attempting to drive a nail with one swing, or splatter the side of a barn with wet paint from a brush.

8: Use Your Rod

Fly rods are usually a good deal more expensive than a run-of-the-mill spinning rod, in part because we are asking a fly rod to do more and be more precise. So let your fly rod do the job you hired it to do. A good rod is like a coiled spring or a drawn longbow—powerful and quietly poised for action. Let the weight of the fly line bend the rod all the way down into the heavier butt section near your hand and then let it unleash that pent-up energy into the fly line. A fly rod is a tool. You paid good money for this tool. Use it.

7: Out of Sight, Out of Mind

Maybe the two best ways to detect glitches in your cast are to either have an honest and critical friend watch your cast or set up a video camera and film your cast and watch it yourself. But that takes forethought and time—or, even rarer, an honest friend. The best way to monitor your cast on the water is to turn your body slightly and watch your backcast. If you can see what you are doing to your fly line, you can compensate and correct. A fairly common mistake is to begin the forward stroke of your cast before the line has fully straightened out on the backcast, causing a sound like a snapping whip. I liken a proper cast to throwing a javelin: It works and it goes far because it is straight. If you turn slightly to verify that it *is* straight, you can chuck that spear to the horizon.

6: Line Pickup

Picking slack fly line off the water before beginning the next cast is the moment most casts begin, and unfortunately also begin to die. The right way to do this is to draw in any of the slack fly line that has gathered on the water in front of you and drop the rod tip low, then pick the entire length of line off the water with the first of your backcasts. The idea is to start out with as much power and control as possible, and get the line moving. If there is a bunch of loose line out on the water, it will take the entire first half of your backward arm motion before the leader and fly are lifted into the air—then there is not enough room and time left to generate enough power to get the line past your head and straight out behind you. All your line will usually end up wrapped around your neck . . . which ruins the Brad Pitt imagery for the cute tourist watching from the bridge.

5: Take a Bow

Drop the rod tip once the job is done. Don't bend at the waist, just dip the rod once your final forward casting stroke (and abrupt stop) have sent the entire line and leader out to the intended target. If you leave the rod tip up at the ten o'clock stop position for too long, the line will come to a jerking halt and bounce back, pulling your fly off target, losing several feet of distance, and causing the rig to pile clumsily onto the water. I have seen the legendary Joe Humphreys perfect this into something he calls the "tuck cast" for plunging weighted nymphs deep and quickly into pocket water. But, as Yogi Berra at some point probably said, *unless you're doing it deliberately, don't do it deliberately.*

4: Line Speed

The reason the term *fast action* is popular verbiage for copywriters working up new catalogs for fly rod companies is because a fast fly rod generates fast line speed, and fast line speed helps make more things possible with any given cast. The right rod allows you to cast farther, cast more efficiently into the wind, use heavier flies, and manage low-hanging branches. But like flying in a supersonic private jet, a fast rod can either get you to the Bellagio really, really fast or run you smack into the side of a mountain before you have a chance to buckle in and flirt with the stewardess. Increased line speed is the primary reason for hauling line. A *haul* is when you pull the fly line with your non-casting hand at the same time you are beginning the next stroke of your cast. If you are adding this line-accelerating pull at the start of both your forward and back stroke, you are achieving what is called a *double haul*. The ability to double haul is hinged almost entirely on timing and rhythm, and is crucial when casting big rods and heavy flies.

3: Letting Go

You can pick your line off the water perfectly, wait until just the right moment to begin your forward casting stroke (even add a well-timed haul!), and stop the rod at just the right spot, and your cast will still travel only half the distance it should if you don't let loose of the fly line and let it shoot out of the rod guides. To do this right, you can't let go of the fly line too soon or too late—timing is everything, as trite as that sounds. Once you stop your final forward casting stroke, let the fly rod straighten out, throwing all of that built-up energy from the bent rod into the fly line, and *just then* bring your line hand up and *let it go!* Let the momentum of the line suck all that loose line at your feet up through the stripping guide and out onto the water. This will not just add a great deal of distance to your cast, it will allow your leader to unroll more gracefully and your fly to arrive at its destination on the water more delicately.

2: Over Casting

Now is the perfect time to revisit that Kirk Deeter quote from the intro of this chapter. The best judge of your casting is the fish. Most beginning fly fishers have difficulties learning to cast, and intermediates struggle to improve on what they have learned. The biggest culprit is not spending enough time with a fly rod in hand— but that can be easily remedied. Casting is not catching, however. I have seen (and worked for in the industry) some guys who had a very accurate and FFF-certified cast, but were embarrassingly poor fishermen. The worst mistake many anglers make once they become comfortable with casting is to cast too much and too far. The more back-and-forth false casting you do before delivering your fly to the fish, the more the odds get stacked in favor of something going awry. *Badly awry.* And the more line you have out on the water, the more the elements (current and wind) can drag your fly, wrap your leader around stuff, and generally cause you not to fool fish.

1: Change It Up

What worked once may not work twice. If the variables change, you must adjust your cast to match the new conditions. The casting stroke you grew accustomed to while fishing your 9-foot, 6-weight Sage broomstick will not serve you well when a friend hands you a soft little 7-foot, 4-weight Garrison bamboo. So every fly rod—like every skipping stone on the river—throws a bit differently. But even the same rod can act one way when paired with a certain fly line and completely differently when paired with another. Heavily weighted streamers require you to use a little bit more of a deliberate hesitation before beginning each casting stroke, sometimes enough time to feel the weight of the heavy fly pull on the line. Then there are the natural obstacles like crosswinds and big willow trees directly behind where you intend to make your stand. Out on the water things are rarely as ideal as they are on a casting lawn.

Chapter 13

The Top Ten Mistakes Made by Novices

This part of the book is not meant to be condescending to the beginning fly fisher. If you recognize yourself or any of your own errors in these ten common pitfalls, relax and take it in as constructive criticism. Also take solace in the knowledge that every single one of us has been the new Jack. Embrace it and learn from it. The more you take in and remember from your first year in the sport, the better

Be careful what you wipe with.

teacher you will be when it is your turn to pass on the torch. And that time will come way sooner than you are expecting ... *trust me.*

10: The Casting Issue

As a novice, you may be intimidated by the prospect of casting a fly rod. Somewhere in your travels you may have seen someone on a lake or big river throwing 80 feet of fly line and making it look cool and graceful, and that undoubtedly is one of the motivating forces pushing you into the sport. Admit it to yourself—it's okay. It looked easy (right?), but when you picked up a rod and attempted to duplicate what you saw, everything collapsed around you like an offensive line that hates the quarterback. But don't cash it in and Craigslist your new gear just yet. There are a slew of common casting mistakes (breaking your wrist, lazy backcasts, slack line between your stripping hand and stripping guide), but you will become proficient in time. Take open-minded advice and get some instruction down at your local fly shop. The biggest and most detrimental problem, however (and the one that often goes unfixed), is the tendency of the novice to cast *too far.* It is hard to get your flies to drift naturally when you have just cast it across 40 feet of changing and conflicting currents. Get closer, make shorter casts, and keep your rod tip high!

9: Poor Preparation

It is hard to be properly prepared for something if you have no clue what you're in for. If you are already a skier or snowboarder and are getting into fly fishing, or maybe you used to hunt some growing up, or did a tour or two in the army, you know the deal. And 90 percent of the deal is having the forethought to bring the proper clothing: a change of undershirt if you are doing something intense, warm clothing if you are drastically changing altitude, and, you know, rain gear if you are spending the day on planet Earth. But being properly prepared for a fishing trip goes a bit beyond these obvious things, like having decent polarized sunglasses, keeping your waders patched and functional, and always having the right tippet and leaders on hand. Don't wait until the night before to attempt a patch job on a scruffy pair of waders you just dug out of the basement, or be the tool who needs to wait until the fly shop opens in the morning to pick up 5X tippet and some dry fly floatant. Oh, I will appreciate your patronage, but your fishing buddies will cuss at you for forcing the late start.

8: Not Reading vs. Reading Too Much

I am often stunned by certain people I speak to about fishing: guys and gals who have never cracked open any of the 1,983 beginning/how-to fly-fishing books out there, or ever googled the words *fly fishing,* but nevertheless here they are, in a busy fly shop in the middle of August, saying, "Excuse me, sir. How do you fly fish?" Maybe the only thing worse than not doing any reading or research whatsoever before wandering onto the firing range is to read too much. Reading every author who has ever penned an opinion about fly selection can freeze your brain. *It don't matter none!* Read only enough—at first—to give yourself the gist. The more you learn on the water about different aspects of the sport, the more questions will be raised. *These* are the questions that can then only be answered by further reading and long conversations in fly shops—or back on the river, where the biggest problems always have to be taken to be solved.

7: Bad Advice

Bad advice seems to find fly-fishing beginners like phone scams find widowed grandmothers. This comes in many forms, from the fly rod that "does everything" and now you have an 8½-foot 6/7-weight, to the 12-inch amnesia butt section connected to the 9-foot leader connected to the 2 feet of extra tippet and now the first-time caster is going to strangle himself with 12 feet of uncontrollable nylon garrote. The best remedy? Find a fly shop or a fishing friend you trust, and always remember that a third of what you hear is total nonsense.

6: Gadgets

Fly fishing has turned into a gadget-driven industry. Look around and take note the next time you are in a fly shop. How many of the little packages pinned to slat board are bursting with trinkets you have not only never seen before, but have no idea what they are used for? Lots, I am sure. And none of them will buy you a fish. Learn the basics. Get good at them. And don't develop an overreliance on gadgets.

5: In Over Your Head

Novice fly fishers have a tendency to get ahead of themselves. I respect this tendency, don't get me wrong . . . It says to me you are eager to learn and love the challenge. But don't beat yourself up too bad if you drove down to the most technical tailwater in the state and had some difficulty. Take the time to master your small-creek home water before you get too carried away with the traveling trout bum lifestyle. Those small creeks and 8-inch browns and brookies can teach you almost all you need to know about fishing. *Almost.*

4: Fear of Knots

Fishermen use line and they tie knots. My earliest memories of my grandfather are the old black-and-whites of him mending commercial fishing nets in the sunny twine fields near Lake Erie. And I guess I was too young to remember my dad teaching me the improved clinch. Knots are a fact of fishing life; in fact, they are a large part of the culture and tradition of every form of fishing I know. I don't know at what point we lost this, it just slowly became a more and more common issue—a fear of knots! There is now a sea of gadgets on the market that claim to chase away these goblins. But just like the Big Bird night light you had as a little kid, these things only pacify—they don't *really* keep away the ghouls. Learn to tie the knots. Simple. You can't fish without them.

3: Time on the Water

"Been gettin' out much?" I ask the guy putzing about the shop on a Saturday morning.

"Naw . . . been too busy this summer," he says.

Okay, what's wrong with this picture? The creek is a four-minute walk from the front cash register! Rather than lament about not having enough time to go fishing, just go fishing. Keep a rod and a small box of flies in your car at all times. Fish before work. Fish after work. Fish before the big game in the afternoon. Every trip to the river does not need to be a daylong adventure—half days are *way* cool. You can choose the best time of day to coincide with the prime fishing, leave yourself plenty of time to get something domestic done around the house, and you aren't exhausted to the point of collapsing on the nice, cold kitchen tile within three steps of returning home. And in the end it is time on the water that will make you a better fly fisher . . . nothing else.

2: Being a Bad Dancer

You can look good and have shiny new shoes, but you can't hide "got no rhythm" once on the dance floor. In the fly-fishing industry, we have what we call LOFT. This is a somewhat colorful term for a "lack of talent." When a customer brings back a top-of-the-line Sage fly rod complaining that it is faulty and tangles up the line when casting, we smile, blame it on LOFT, and take him out back for a free casting lesson. But being a good fly fisher goes so much farther than an ability to cast without killing yourself. You need to be comfortable with your tools, on the water and in your own body. You have to have an element or two of grace and athleticism . . . It *is* a sport, after all. Klutzy footwork knocks rocks into pools and spooks trout. On the other hand, supervised slow dancing at the spring formal doesn't always get the job done either—sometimes moving fast and covering more water in a shorter period of time is the best way to score.

1: The Wrong Attitude

You have to be a little bit hungry to become a good angler, and while fishing is a fun and relaxing pastime, fishing *well* is a serious endeavor. If you want to become good at it, you need to treat it as such. Treat the fish you are after like the wild creatures they are, and when you strike out or get frustrated with yourself, don't lose your mind—it is *supposed* to be hard. *Embrace it!*

Chapter 14

The Top Ten Ways to Take Better Fishing Photos

We fishermen have been attempting to capture the memory of our catch since the beginning of mankind. Fortunately, we are no longer left to paint our prey on cave walls. Since the invention of the camera, the perfect "grip and grin" photo has evolved into a true art. We want to capture all aspects of that great moment in time. We want to

Garrison Doctor with a fine steelhead on the Stillwater River in Idaho.
BIRCH FETT, REPYOURWATER.COM

be reminded of our mood, our choice of equipment for the day, our surroundings, the weather, and, of course, our prize—the fish! This section will help you take better fishing photos. Your friends may even thank you.

10: Preparation

Always be prepared to either take a magazine cover photo or be the one on the cover. Dress like you know how to fish. You don't have to always be clean-shaven and snazzed to the nines, but a haircut and nice shirt are a great idea. Always fish with a partner who also carries a decent camera, knows how to use it, and is willing to stop casting to do so. If your favorite fishing partners are lacking in any of these departments, send them this book! Also, if a rifle without ammo is just a club (as they say in the army), then a camera without film is just a rock. Charge it up the night before, and be sure the memory card has space available.

9: Stop and Poke at Bugs

If the fishing action is slow, take time out to smell the flowers (and then photograph them). Take plenty of shots of the local flora and fauna. Close-up photos of the aquatic bugs hatching on the stream that day are always of interest to fly fishers. These photos are great to have as reference during a long winter at the tying bench, or if you are ever in need of material for an entomology presentation. Also, it is not a bad idea to snap a quick shot of the last of those hot flies that are working so well—you are bound to lose that last one, and the poor guy at your local fly shop will appreciate a photo and not a vague description of a small, brown, fuzzy-lookin' thing. So choose a camera with a good macro setting.

8: Postcard Moments

Pay close attention to your fishing partner during your day on the water. Never pass on the opportunity to take that "postcard pic." Few photos capture a sense of place better, and these are usually the photos that other anglers enjoy the most. The person in the photo is only a small element of the overall scene and is often unidentifiable, thus allowing the viewer to impose himself into the picture. Paying attention to your partner also enables you to be Johnny-on-the-spot when he or she eventually hooks into that trophy fish.

7: Bent Rods

Do your best to capture the action and thrill of the fight. This is one of the hardest photos to get perfect, because it often happens quickly and neither you nor your fishing partner has much control over the situation. The number one detail that must always be featured prominently in a "fighting shot" is the bent rod. The entire rod needs to be in the frame (ideally silhouetted against a light background) and both fighters need to be present. The fisherman is easy—get at least his upper torso in the frame—but the fish is harder. Rarely will you be able to snap the shot just as the fish is jumping, but attempt to capture the point where the line enters the water. If the water is clear enough to see the shape of the fish, or if it is splashing on the surface, your photo will be even better.

During a lull in a long fight, encourage your fisherman to put the fish on the reel (reel in excess fly line). Some line hanging loose over a knee or rock looks cool, but 40 feet of it wrapped around cattails and wading boots looks ridiculous. There will not be time to reel in this line once the fish is landed. Also, during the fight the photographer should be formulating a game plan. *Where is the sun?* The sun should always be at the photographer's back. *What will make the most interesting background?* We want to get a feel for where the fish was caught. *Will this photo desperately need some color because the fisherman is wearing drab clothing? Will I need the flash on or off? Have I turned off the macro from that last shot of the green drake mayfly?* The camera should be ready and the photographer in the proper position.

6: Remove Those Sunglasses

The protagonist in a great fishing success photo should not look like the sunken-eyed spawn of the underworld. There is a ton of personality and emotion emitted from the eyes. We want to see that—it makes better photos. The problem is that almost all of us fish with the aid of polarized optics . . . as we should. If you have just hooked a decent fish and your fishing partner is at the ready, take the time during a lull in the fight to pocket those sunnies. If you *are* the partner, wait until the fisherman has the fish hoisted, then lean in and pluck them off his face. Trust me, he will be powerless to stop you—he has his hands full!

5: Fill Flash

Do not forget the importance of a fill flash. This enables you to see your angler's face in harsh sun under a long or wide-brimmed hat. We have all seen dark, featureless mystery-hero shots—or too much shadow in the eyes, too much contrast. The fill flash icon on most cameras looks like a lightning bolt, but is usually not the auto flash setting. But be sure you are in range! Most flashes can only properly reach out to about 10 feet.

4: The Money Shot

The ultimate grip and grin . . . the money shot . . . the photo your buddy will have blown up, framed, and hung in the living room. Consistently getting great shots has much to do with proper teamwork and communication. If you and your fishing partner are properly equipped and prepared to assume either the role of fisherman or photographer at a moment's notice, you will have success. As the fisherman, your responsibilities are to mind the fly line, remove your hood (if you're wearing a jacket), and tell the photographer where you would like to land the fish. Once you land the fish, your only tasks are to keep the fish clean (no mud or leaves), keep your hands off the photo side of the fish, and smile. Once the fish is out of the water, the clock is ticking. Do everything your photographer tells you. But remember, the photo of a fish of a lifetime is never worth the life of a fish of a lifetime. Treat the fish gently, and get it back into the water within seconds.

3: More Spots, Less Knuckles

As the photographer, your moment to shine begins when the fish is brought to hand. You should only take enough time to get three quick shots before the fish is released. Think fast and act faster. Check to see that the face of your fisherman is not in shadow. Have him turn or even move into the sun. Reach out and adjust his collar or lift up the bill of his ball cap. Whoop it up a bit if you have to. Get your fisherman to show some emotion! Leave plenty of border—you always want room to crop later on. Never scalp your fisherman! Get all of his head in the frame. Try to get the fly rod and reel in the photo. You may have to prop the rod up against your subject, or stick it under his arm. Make sure no mud or leaves are on the fish—this was the fisherman's job, but now he should be looking at you, not the fish. Lastly, encourage him to hold the fish up and out. He'll want the memory to be 2 inches bigger, not 2 inches smaller.

2: Don't Forget the Fish

Take photos of the fish, not just the fisherman. This becomes more important if the catch happens to be less than gigantic. The fish may still be a memorable trophy: a 14-inch brown trout from your favorite small stream taken on a dry fly, or a breathtaking little cutthroat from a high-altitude lake most people never dare hike. In these cases it becomes important to focus on the fish. Only resort to the "another fish in the grass" shot if you are alone. Remember, we want the human element in these photos. Know the difference between a photo of a fish and a fishing photo! Also, second only to a human face, a human hand exhibits the most personality—and as Martha Stewart says, "That's a good thing."

1: And . . . the Release!

Never pass on the opportunity of a "release" shot. The criteria for a good release shot is a bit different than your typical grip-and-grin or fighting shot. Similar to the "fish in hand" shot, the main focus should be the fish, but the entire personality of the fisherman should be present. We should only see the important parts of the person but feel as though we can see all of him. We should not notice that all that is in the photo is the forearm and side of the face. We can see the emotion and the action. After all, this is when the fisherman is letting go. He is relinquishing control of the fish as well as the center of attention. For the same reasons it is also important that the fish be partially in the water, but not so far as to obscure the open eye of the fish. We want its personality, too!

Chapter 15

The Top Ten Trout Dry Flies

A fly fisherman casting a dry fly over a scenic western trout stream may be the most pure and romantic image in all of the sport. Many of us were lured into fly fishing because of imagery like this . . . or writings that describe such scenes. Some of us still choose to fish this exact way, without deviation, even if the trout are not rising. It may be the closest to honest way to catch a trout. *Maybe.* But isn't that what's said behind our backs? *Fishermen are born honest, but they all get over it.* Listed here are the ten most honest flies you can have in your box.

10: Stimulator

The origins of this big, bushy dry fly can be traced back to the 1940s, although it got tweaked in the 1950s to the elk-hair-rich fly we still fish to this day. Many fly tiers have made their own alterations since then—attempting to attach their names to this pattern. The Stimulator (or Super Improved Mini-Sofa Pillow) has as much buoyant elk hair tied in and stiff-fibered hackle wound on as possible. It is a versatile fly that comes in many sizes and colors and can be used to imitate anything from large adult caddis and stoneflies to some rubber-legged variation that will be mistaken for a struggling grasshopper.

9: Clown Shoe Caddis

The distinctive clump of fluorescent cerise foam on the Clown Shoe Caddis makes this fly the most visible caddis available. It is a superb, workhorse dry fly that can act as a mule for a couple heavy dropper

The Clown Shoe Caddis floats like a cork and is easily visible.

nymphs in rough water. The low-slung abdomen forces it to ride correctly every time—even when rigged without a dropper. The Clown Shoe is an exceptionally buoyant dry fly as a result of two ingredients: the proportionally gigantic clump of elk hair tied in as the wing, and the highly visible McFly Foam post at the top. This hot pink color is the easiest to detect on broken water or during odd light conditions, and the gaudiness actually increases the effectiveness of the fly.

8: Amy's Ant

This fly is suggestive enough to be fished as an adult stonefly or large caddis, as well as a grasshopper or cicada. The Amy's Ant is a favorite of guides up and down the Rocky Mountains because of its tendency to bring large trout to the surface. It is a perfect joining of all the best and buggiest natural materials—elements such as dubbing, hackle, and elk hair—and synthetics like foam, rubber legs, and flashy chenille. The Amy's Ant hit the scene in the late 1990s around Jackson Hole, Wyoming, and now can be found in fly shops all over the country in sizes as large as #8 and as small as #14.

7: RS2

The RS2, or Rim's Semblance 2, was created in the early 1970s for the selective trout in Colorado's South Platte River. This tiny wisp of a fly was originated by Rim Chung, who claims not to be a fly tier and—ironically—never intended his fly to be dry fly. The sparseness of the RS2 makes it a superb imitation of a wide range of mayfly nymphs, but its size and lightness make it a ready dry fly for the most fickle tailwater risers.

6: Missing Link

First tied as a caddis dry fly for the Lower Sacramento River in California, the Missing Link has developed into an every-possible-insect imitator. Large olive ones are used as green drakes, smaller ones in the same color are used as *Baetis* adults, and others are tied to mimic yellow sally stoneflies and tricos. The list goes on. This fly has only been around for a few years, but has captured every dry-fly fisherman's attention because it looks buggy, floats well, and fools trout more often than not.

5: Curmudgeon Crumpler

This may be the best trout dry fly you have yet heard about. The Crumpler was originally created in an attempt to mimic large, gangly crane flies hatching in the high lakes of Colorado's Indian Peaks Wilderness Area, but soon morphed into a more compact, hardy

The Curmudgeon Crumpler is a great cricket fly pattern.

fly resembling a cricket or small grasshopper. This fly is tied on an Umpqua C300BL barbless competition hook, so it has a very organic curve and an extended spear to hold trout without damaging them. This is my favorite fly to fish small, wild trout streams.

4: Comparadun

This dry fly has a boring name but the most fun and interesting history and lineage of any fly I know. In the 1940s a trapper in New York's Adirondack Mountains lashed deer hair onto a hook and caught trout. A high-school-aged boy saw this and was impressed, and later goes on to invent a dry fly called the Haystack. Fast-forward to the mid-1970s and another man takes this idea, tightens it up a bit—makes it slimmer and sparser—and we now have the dry known to all fly fishers as the Comparadun. It is a simple fly consisting of nothing more than fine, black-tipped deer hair, dubbing, and slim hackle-fibers for tails, but it's the lifelike silhouette and buoyancy that make it a winner.

3: Beetle

Trout are suckers for a beetle—*any* beetle! Any given fly shop carries a dozen or so different beetle patterns, but the overriding common denominator is the color: black. And they have to be buggy and buoyant, too. Without the aid of dense hackle or large clumps of elk hair, the buoyancy issue is a hard obstacle to overcome. That is why most beetle fly patterns are tied with black foam and a few small rubber legs protruding out the sides. It works. I do, however, respect a little bit more than the others any beetle that is tied without foam.

2: Elk Hair Caddis

Created on Loyalsock Creek in Pennsylvania, the Elk Hair Caddis is the best known and most used caddis dry fly in the country. In fact, given its simplicity and effectiveness, it is the standard that all other adult caddisfly imitations are held to. The Elk Hair Caddis pattern is tied to a straight-shanked dry fly hook and calls for thin wire ribbing, palmered dry fly hackle, dubbing, and a healthy clump of the namesake elk hair on top for the wing. This fly can be drifted or skittered on the surface of the water to imitate either the hatching adult or the egg-laying female.

1: Parachute Adams

Possibly the best-known fly of all, the original Adams dry fly was first tied by Leonard Halladay in 1922 for his close friend Charles Adams to fish for the wily brown trout planted in Michigan's Boardman River.

The Parachute Adams is the most popular mayfly pattern available today.

The fly Halladay created was a down-winged dry meant to imitate a caddis adult, but evolved into a fly with collared hackle and a long tail meant to imitate an adult mayfly. About ten years after the invention of the Adams, there emerged a new style of dry flies called *parachutes* where the hackle is wound around a piece of material protruding off the hook shank (now commonly called a *post*) instead of the hook shank itself. The typically white post made any dry fly tied in this manner much easier for an angler to see on the water and made the imprint of the fly more realistic as it sits in the surface film of the water. There are many fly fishers who claim that if they were allowed only one fly to fish for the rest of their years, it would be this one.

Chapter 16

The Top Ten Trout Nymphs

The vast majority of what a trout puts in its mouth are aquatic insects, and an equally vast majority of these bugs' lives are spent under river rocks or bouncing and crawling around between these rocks. Hence the submerged trout nymph is unarguably the most important object in a trout fisherman's fly box. There are many different species of these aquatic insects, though, and there are even more flies tied to emulate them. Here are the best nymph fly patterns you can have in your box.

10: Girdle Bug

This large, weighted nymph was originally tied to fish the Big Hole River in the 1930s and has been such a successful and popular fly that it has spawned many replications and spin-offs. I have seen this general pattern at various fly shops over the years, all named differently: Pickle, Cat Turd, Knotty Girl, Pat's Rubberlegs, McGinnis Rubberlegs, McKee's Rubberlegs, Randy's Rubberlegs. They are all the same fly, but with very slight variations on the theme. They are simple and suggestive flies tied with nothing but lead wire, several sets of rubber legs, and an entire body of chenille. The Girdle Bug is able to be a large stonefly, hellgrammite, crane fly, or even (if retrieved erratically) a fleeing crayfish. I prefer the Randy's version because it is tied with subtle yet slightly flashy chenille and on a bent shank hook to let the lead underwrap off-balance the fly—this forces the hook point to ride up, keeping snags minimal.

9: Copper John

The #16 red-bodied Copper John is the best-selling fly of any kind in the last two decades. Here is a nymph that set the standard for what a fly could be, not so much as an ultra-realistic imitation (it has the general body shape of a mayfly nymph in smaller sizes and a stonefly in larger sizes), but as a heavy, bead-headed attractor nymph. The original, copper-bodied version of this fly in a #18 has been a go-to at some point for almost every fly fisherman I have known.

8: Banksia Bug

This fly imitates the masses of free-living caddis larvae found in trout streams all over the West. It's a very productive fly, probably because this particular caddis larva is a notoriously poor swimmer, often getting swept away in the current, making it an easily recognizable food organism that constitutes a large portion of a trout's diet. I have found this pattern to work well in rivers with an abundance of small to medium-size stonefly nymphs, leading me to believe the Banksia Bug is suggestive enough for trout to mistake it for any number of long-bodied aquatic insects. With this in mind, I am now using this fly in lakes with equal success.

7: Rainbow Warrior

This super-flashy attractor nymph amplifies the lessons learned from flies such as the Copper John about the effective triggers that make a trout eat. The Rainbow Warrior is tied on a curved-shank hook, has a tungsten bead at the head (to make it sink superfast), and is tied with enough opal tinsel wrapped around the body to make the thing look like a flashbulb underwater. It gets the attention of every trout in the run, and trout tend to eat little things that get their attention and look alive!

A box full of heavily weighted Banksia Bugs.

6: Jujubaetis

The blue-winged olive, or BWO, is one of (if not *the*) most important mayfly to a fly fisher. They can be found on almost all trout streams and—if given the right weather—can hatch (and be eaten!) pretty much year-round. But these mayflies are small and slim, and the usual, run-of-the-mill nymph just is not going to cut it when the water is clear and the trout want BWOs for breakfast. The diminutive teardrop shape of the Jujubaetis perfectly matches the natural *Baetis* nymphs. A realistic silhouette is the key when you are after finicky trout. I use the unweighted version when I have this fly incorporated with an already weighted, multi-nymph rig,

The Jujubaetis is a must-have in any fly box.

but choose the Jujubaetis tied with a tiny black tungsten bead when I have the nymph hanging below a dry fly.

5: Prince

This fly was created on the Kings River in California in the early 1940s, and the bead-head version has become an ever-increasing staple in the fly collection of nymph fishermen everywhere. The original Prince Nymph was tied using black ostrich herl for the body, but now is tied using peacock herl to take advantage of the natural, attractive iridescence of that material—much like the Pennsylvania-born Zug Bug and the Colorado-born Twenty Incher. All three of these patterns make for fantastic small stonefly imitations, as well as green drake nymphs.

4: Zebra Midge

There may be a million and five midge pupa patterns out there in the blogs, books, websites, and fly bins, and they all work and I love them all. I just flat-out love midge pupae. This bug (more precisely, *this stage in the life* of this bug) makes up the bulk of the diet of practically every trout in the world. They are very, *very* plentiful. So out of all these masses of midge fly patterns—that all look very similar—which is best? I guess when I am confronted with the smartest (i.e., wariest) of trout, I dig in my box for the slim, neutrally buoyant, super-realistic, *Jujube-esque* flies, and they work when I need them. But honestly, many of the trout I fish for are not tailwater savvy—they eat Zebra Midges, the fast food of the fly-tying world. Over 100 billion served. Nothing but a #20 curved-shank hook, bead at the front, and black-thread body ribbed with silver wire . . . a cheap, drive-through Happy Meal.

3: Micro May

This mayfly nymph pattern was conceived in the fast-water sections of the Madison River in Montana. The Micro May is a petite nymph, but has a large bead-head to get the fly down where it needs to be in order to be an effective river nymph. I rely heavily on this fly to get me through the seasons because it comes in so many desirable flavors. I have the *Baetis* version as well as the PMD (pale morning dun) and *Callibaetis* Micro Mays at the ready during the appropriate times of year.

2: Two-Bit Hooker

I strongly believe this fly is the best of the new-generation flies now available to us as fly fishers. The Two-Bit Hooker takes into consideration and solves all the problems of the modern, technical nympher. The Two-Bit has a realistic, slender profile coupled with the weight of *two* small tungsten beads—which allow it to maintain its fine figure. Its small size yet extreme weight make it a perfect dry-dropper pattern as well as a great confidence pattern in any deep, multi-fly nymph rig.

1: Pheasant Tail

Well, you knew the number one nymph had to be this or the Gold-Ribbed Hare's Ear, didn't ya? Well, the Hare's Ear just didn't make the cut. Sorry. Back off. This is my list, so I get to pick. The origin of the PT Nymph, as it is now commonly referred to in fishing reports nationwide, is on the chalk streams of southern England, and it is considered by many to be the oldest of the modern nymphs. The fly you all know now—and most likely already own—is the version that has been improved and reborn in the States. The Pheasant Tail is sold in every fly shop I have ever entered, and will catch trout until the day trout kick the bug habit. Period.

Chapter 17

The Top Ten Trout Streamers

Streamer fishing is a fast-paced and exciting way to target trout. It may not always be the most productive method, but it's usually the best way to single out the biggest, meanest, most cannibalistic monsters in the creek. Many avid fly fishers who have only spent time on creeks and small rivers prospecting for trout are still scared of big hooks and big flies. That is okay. If it is an infrequent trick, it has a better chance of working. When a fish sees prey larger than what could possibly fit on a #12 hook, it is almost *always* safe to pounce! And always beneficial, as they can then skulk at the bottom of the river for the next two days digesting the spoils of war like a fat uncle on Thanksgiving afternoon—a two-day reprieve from darting about frantically after midge pupae. For the hard-core streamer fisherman, there are gigantic, double-articulated flies that are almost as much fun to strip in as an actual trout. But here are the ten best single-hook streamer flies that have been proven over time and will break you in nicely to the cult of the trout streamer.

10: Gray Ghost

The Gray Ghost is a legendary fly first tied as a smelt imitation to fool Maine's large brook trout, and although this pattern is nearly ninety years old, there are few better. Several materials are used in this fly's recipe, as was the tradition of the day (largely influenced by the English fully dressed salmon flies), but the most distinctive ingredients are long strands of peacock and white bucktail on the belly, gray rooster feathers over the top, a set of silver pheasant-body feathers up front as the "shoulders," and, of course, the ever-present jungle cock "cheek." It wasn't this streamer alone that earned a place in angling history and this top ten list, but more the impact the creator, Carrie Stevens, had on the designs and methods of tying trout streamers. She drew from old-world elegance and added a new-world mindset to create natural action and imitation in her flies. Some thirty years before the likes of Lefty Kreh and Bob Clouser would take the handoff and advance the ball, a woman from Rangeley, Maine, redefined streamer flies and set the bar for the rest of us to follow.

9: Autumn Splendor

A newer streamer, the Autumn Splendor is a genetic cross between the Girdle Bug and a cone-head Woolly Bugger tied in a combination of brown, orange, and yellow. This streamer was concocted in Colorado's Roaring Fork Valley in the early 1990s and is now a go-to streamer to be cast to the banks from a drift boat and stripped fast. The Autumn Splendor is just the right size, shape, and color to look enough like a large stonefly nymph to work exceptionally well dead-drifted on an upstream cast before being stripped in like a sculpin or crayfish on the downstream swing.

8: Sculpzilla

The Sculpzilla is a heavy streamer that by shape and size alone looks like a run-of-the-mill cone-head Zonker-style sculpin imitation, but the strip of rabbit fur over the back of this fly has much more movement in the water than it should. This is because the Sculpzilla is articulated: The big weighted cone at the head (a cone with eyeballs, ooh wee!) is mounted on the front hook, which is clipped off at the bend, and a supersharp Gamakatsu stinger hook is trailing in the back. This is a great fly to start fishing or tying, as it is a gateway drug into the deeper and more sinister world of big articulated streamers.

There is just nothing kind about a Sculpzilla.

7: Platte River Spider

This fly is very effective at taking good trout in moving water, but is a rare sort of streamer. The Platte River Spider is a relatively new design, but is dressed with the wisdom and tradition of flies much more classic, tried, and proven. The Spider was born in the mid-1990s, a little on the Rio Grande and a bit on the North Platte, and was influenced further by forays into steelhead country and culture to the north and west. Whereas most modern streamers are tied with as much lead wire wrapped around the shank as possible, or tungsten cones and heavy dumbbell eyes strapped to the head, this fly deliberately and against the grain goes weightless. The idea is a simple and proven concept: Impressionistic flies that suggest life are more effective, and in nature, movement equals life. This pattern is tied with natural materials that are readily available, affordable, and, most importantly, breathe with movement. Cast the Spider with a sinking or sink-tip line and allow the fly to move and respond to each subtle variation of current.

6: Sparkle Minnow

There could not be a better or more accurately descriptive name for this fly. The Sparkle Minnow does not scrimp on the bling. At first glance, a fly tier might assume there is an entire pack of golden Angel Hair and pearl Ice Dub wound onto a big straight-shanked streamer hook. This fly was first tied back in 1995 for smallmouth bass in the creeks and small rivers of central Illinois, but rapidly began adding other notches to the bedpost. White bass, stripers, walleyes, and muskies fell to the lure of the Sparkle Minnow. Now it is used for Pacific salmon and is a very popular streamer in the western "trout states" for big browns and rainbows. There is at least one guide service in Montana that refers to this fly as the Ramp-to-Ramp, as it is often the only streamer they have on their clients' rods from the put-in ramp to the take-out ramp. Swinging a Sparkle Minnow in the current or stripping it rhythmically in slow/still waters is often all that is needed. Sometimes, the less you move it, the better it seems to work.

5: Near Nuff Sculpin

The Near Nuff is a sculpin-imitating streamer tied on a standard, straight-shanked, down-eyed streamer hook with heavy lead dumbbell eyes mounted on the front to not only sink the fly to the bottom (where sculpin tend to be), but also add enough weight to flip the hook over in the water, causing it to swim with the hook point up and away from potential snags. Once a weighted streamer such as this turns over, the down-turned eye sticks up at a 45-degree angle toward the angler, essentially turning the streamer into a miniature jig. The

Near Nuff Sculpin is tied in mottled tan and olive, and is very realistic in the water.

4: Belly Ache Minnow

This streamer is stunningly realistic and will make fishermen want to lay their wet fly on a rock next to a real minnow for one of those cool "look, we matched the hatch!" photos. The Belly Ache is not a complicated fly and does not have so much going on that it can't be taken seriously by serious anglers. The Belly Ache *does* have a bit of very creative hydro-engineering going on underneath the rabbit-strip top and flashy Ice Dub belly. Mounted onto the Gamakatsu SC15 saltwater hook is a ribbed tungsten fly weight originally designed

A handful of Belly Ache Minnows.

to be tied as the weighted base for Czech-style anchor nymphs and scuds. It is the perfect way to turn this baitfish streamer into a deep, snagless minnow. I have personally landed almost every freshwater fish species (both warm-water and trout) on this fly, in either the #1/0 and, my favorite, the #4 "baby ache."

3: Woolly Bugger

The Woolly Bugger is unarguably the best known and most universally used trout streamer of the last half century. It is tied and sold in about every size, color, and configuration imaginable—as a weighted steamer with lead wire, colored beads, or heavy cone-heads to simulate anything from a dragonfly nymph, crayfish, or leech to a small baitfish. Some versions are subtle in design, while others have gaudy flash and rubber legs tied into the marabou tail or chenille and palmered hackle body. Like so many of the best trout streamers, the Woolly Bugger was first tied to be a smallmouth bass fly. The first Buggers were made in the late 1960s to mimic the hellgrammites (dobsonfly larvae) found in many Pennsylvania rivers, but the pattern did not become well-known until the mid-1980s.

2: Muddler Minnow

The first fly I ever tied onto a beat-up leader and cast with an old hand-me-down fiberglass fly rod was a Muddler Minnow. This classic streamer was born on the banks of the Nipigon River in Ontario in the 1930s, and was a sculpin imitation intended to fool the large resident brook trout. Like any good fly pattern, it has undergone countless generations of alterations and tweaking. The version of the Muddler Minnow commonly fished these days is a tidier and more refined rendition of the simpler and slightly mussed original. Muddlers now have two sets of matched turkey-quill slips as the tail and "wing" on top, gold flat braid over the hook shank as the body, a tan calf-tail "underwing," a deer-hair collar, and a very condensed, well-packed head trimmed out of the wildly flared, but fat, butt ends of the deer hair. Some modern variations have brightly colored marabou as the underwing and a heavy brass cone at the very head.

1: Pine Squirrel Leech

Trout have a serious weakness for leeches. The affinity is so bad that an angler almost can't go wrong with even a poorly tied attempt at a leech imitation. If it *sort of* looks like a leech, there will be trout somewhere willing to eat it. Because of this, there are an absolute ton of various types of leech-esque flies on the market. Some of these streamers are tied using nothing but dark, long-fibered dubbing material, while others utilize long black marabou. The best ones are those tied with a simple, slender length of black pine squirrel. The long guard hairs and dense but soft underfur have the best and most seductive undulating movement underwater, and the hide is thick enough to hold up to being battered around while soft and waterlogged. In creeks, rivers, or high lakes, a Pine Squirrel Leech will make you look like you know what you're doing!

Chapter 18

The Top Ten Warm-Water Flies

It has been put forth that the rise of the urban or warm-water angler has to do with the decline of our economy. This is presuming we cannot afford to chase "real" sport fish, so we are forced to catch bass out of water hazards and carp out of irrigation ditches. *Whatever.* I don't buy any of it. A modern warm-water angler does not pursue the fish he does out of desperation. He does it because he is the new breed of cool. I have good friends, doctors and dentists with quite successful practices, who are lucky enough to afford multiple saltwater fly-fishing vacations a year. These guys now chase carp in the mudflats with the same gusto and enthusiasm as they do with permit and redfish. I also know fly-fishing guides who spend in excess of 150 days chasing trout, and who choose to wash a particularly frustrating day on the trout stream off the books (so to speak) by spending the evening with some cold PBR at a semisecret bass pond. And I know this may be hard for the old guard—what is left of the cane and tweed crowd—but the urban, warm-water fly fisher may be one of the more noticeable of the contemporary guidon-bearers for our sport. They are the best ambassadors as well. They are the fishermen who are seen by the kids on the school bus, from the park swing, and looked down on from atop a bridge or a skateboard. The urban angler is the only one who has a chance of convincing a kid that being outside is okay and maybe (just maybe) a fly rod might be a bit cooler than some Wii game piece. So, I salute and celebrate all of you fellows of the mudflats, brothers of the bass ponds . . . and here are the best flies out there.

10: Flashtail Whistler

The Flashtail Whistler is a large, flashy, eye-catching streamer originally designed for snook, but is a staple fly pattern in all the best pike fishermen's boxes. Pike are extremely predatory and aggressive fish eaters with poor eyesight, making easy targets for the suggestive and erratic behavior of this fly.

9: Geezus Lizard

This fly is modeled after conventional lures like the Pig-n-Jig, only using crosscut rabbit strips and rubber legs. The only slight modifications are the true jig-style hook and the wire-ribbed scud back on the underneath of the fly. This does two things: It makes the fly look a lot cooler and, on the practical side, allows the fly to zip right back down to the mud after it has been jerked by the angler. This gives the fly a very distinctive action in the water, very closely matching the way a spooked crayfish darts out, then immediately tucks back to the bottom. The Geezus Lizard is used primarily for largemouth bass in larger lakes and reservoirs, but it has been a devastating fly for picky northern pike as well as smallmouth bass in deep, swift rivers.

8: Charlie's Airhead

It is hard for me not to compare our cutting-edge streamer flies with their old-school conventional lure contemporaries. So I will just go ahead and do so. In many instances, flies and fly design got hung up in too much tradition and failed to evolve at the same rate as spin- and bait-casting plugs and lures. This may be why it has only been recently that warm-water fly fishers could hold their own alongside their mono-spewing brethren. It's flies like Charlie's Airhead that help even the playing field. Tied on a heavy leader with a loop knot, this fly has the same crazy, walk-the-dog action as the old-favorite Zara Spook lure.

7: Backstabber

The best carp flies are sparse, simply tied, and usually about 1 to 1¾ inches long. Most are weighted, but only slightly (they need to sink but also land in the water quietly). The Backstabber is tied so that the hook point rides up to help resist snagging in shallow water. The most effective colors in this pattern are black, dark olive, brown, and rusty brown. Few carp flies are obvious mimics of something in nature, but are very suggestive once they are fished. This fly can look like a damselfly nymph, crayfish, leech, or anything else a carp might fancy. The brilliance of this suggestive fly pattern is not in the absence of painstaking detail, but in the liveliness, or animation, once it is wet. This fly works because it takes advantage of a very intelligent fish's imagination.

6: Meat Whistle

This is a simple yet suggestive fly pattern utilizing the undulating characteristics of rabbit hide and rubber legs to their full, fish-enticing potential. This makes the Meat Whistle an outstanding fish-catching tool; however, it is not what sets it apart and above other warm-water flies. The Meat Whistle is one of the first streamers to utilize the jig-style hook. The importance of this cannot be overstated, as much of bass fishing success comes from a fisherman's ability to get a weighted fly down to the bottom of a lake in and around submerged stumps, logs, and other structure without getting snagged.

5: Near Nuff Crayfish

If there are a thousand grasshopper flies in existence, then there are a million crayfish imitations out there. I guess it's because these freshwater crustaceans are fun to look at and even more fun to emulate. They have eyes and antennae and legs and big pinchers. Yeah, every fly tier I have ever met is in some way or another obsessed with re-creating the most awesome and lifelike set of pincers on their superimproved signature crayfish fly pattern. *Yawn.* Lions prefer crippled gazelles, and bass prefer defenseless crayfish (i.e., no pincers). Realistic crayfish flies should be judged while swimming, not while resting in a fly box. And the Near Nuff is the best.

4: Booby Frog

The genre of fly most commonly cast to largemouth bass is the topwater "bass bug." They are usually cheaply crafted hunks of cork

By riding point up, the Booby Frog avoids the necessity for weed guards.

or spun deer hair with a few token rubber legs and wisps of chicken tail. These flies are meant to imitate frogs swimming on the surface of a pond. They will work, but not always, and not so well with heavily pressured fish. The Booby Frog does two things: (1) It realistically mimics the appearance and swimming motion of a real frog just below (and peeking out of) the water, and (2) it is one of the few topwater bass flies that are designed to ride hook point up, eliminating the need for cumbersome and obtrusive mono weed guards. This fly is easily the deadliest topwater I have ever fished.

3: Texas Ringworm

This is the fly equivalent to the Texas-rigged rubber worm—one of the most commonly and effectively used tricks in conventional bass fishing. The Texas Ringworm incorporates a long ferruled dubbing loop tail with an internal hook mechanism built using a hard-mono loop that keeps the large but thin-wire hook facing up and snag-free. The hook stays in place even through long or brutal casting, but detaches immediately once a bass takes and the hook is set. Once the fish has been detached, the hard-mono loop is easily reattached. This fly is absolutely deadly. It is best fished with floating line when on small bass ponds and on a sink-tip line when on rivers or larger reservoirs.

2: Dahlberg's Diver

This large and disruptive topwater fly has set a high standard in warm-water flies. Dahlberg's Diver is tied with liberal amounts of marabou, hackle feathers, and Flashabou making up the body of the fly, and a very distinctively shaped head consisting of spun and trimmed deer hair. This fly is designed to dive below the surface during the retrieve and then immediately return to the surface during any pauses or lulls in the retrieve. This action is indicative of sickly or injured fish, thus

The Texas Ringworm is the deadliest bass fly I have ever fished. Use a 1X leader and a loop knot to get the best action.

drawing aggressive strikes from any number of large predators such as bass, northern pike, and muskie.

1: Clouser Minnow

This weighted version of a bucktail streamer may be the most important warm-water fly ever conceived. Originally tied for smallmouth bass in the Susquehanna River, it is a simple, sturdy, and incredibly effective baitfish imitation. More importantly, this fly pattern has had the same degree of influence on contemporary warm-water and streamer flies as Bob Dylan has had on modern music and song writing. The Clouser Minnow can be tied or purchased in several sizes and countless color combinations, depending on the body of water or species being targeted—however, the overall crowd favorite is chartreuse and white.

Chapter 19

The Top Ten Saltwater Flies

The acceptance and rapid gain in the popularity of saltwater fishing has done great things for the world of fly fishing. Not that long ago it was even being touted as the savior of the industry. At a time when fewer and fewer new faces were showing up in fly shops—or more importantly, less money was being spent on new gear—there emerged a phenomenal excuse to buy a top-of-the-line 9-weight and a heavy-duty reel, and take a vacation. It would be to a warm, tropical locale with a mai tai and a beach nearby, too, so the non-fishing side of the family would still assume all was normal. Whether or not saltwater fishing did actually "save" the fly-fishing industry or not is up for debate, but what it did do was add a bit of much-needed excitement to the previously low-key atmosphere of fly fishing. The salt water opened our eyes to new fish species and maybe made some of us better fishermen, or at least better casters. And it opened the door to an entirely new genre of flies. Here are the ten best must-haves if you want in on the action.

10: Reducer

This is one of the newer baitfish streamers being used in salt water, but some incredible success stories are already beginning to pile up. The Reducer was originally designed as a peacock bass fly that is lightweight but has a lot of bulk and a wide face to push a ton of water. It's also become popular with the offshore fly anglers. This fly is tied with feathers off the back, deer hair splayed out to form a head, and two oversize 3-D eyes. The larger-size Reducer is used for sailfish, and the smaller versions are carried by striper and blue fishermen on the East Coast and rooster and jack fishermen on the West Coast.

9: Chili Pepper Worm

The "worm hatch" on the eastern coast of the United States and down as far south as Cuba is fast becoming a well-known and important phenomenon in saltwater fly fishing. Each year in late May and into early June, the palolo worms (a saltwater invertebrate roughly the size of your index finger) cut loose from their coral-rock home and swim with a sense of purpose for the reef offshore. These hatches occur in the late afternoon and last until dark, often launching fish species of every shape and size into a feeding frenzy. All spring tarpon fishermen in the Florida Keys carry a few worm flies and keep a lookout for the first of these neon-red creatures to zip by under the bow. Tarpon can lose all inhibitions during these hatches and sometimes get very close to the boat even with the engine running, but they still can be very selective and only eat those flies that look most like the natural. The Chili Pepper Worm is a simple fly using nothing but a ferruled dubbing loop tied on a sturdy hook, but it looks and swims and glows just like the real McCoy.

8: Megalopsicle

There is a special sect of saltwater fly fishers who revel in the remoteness and possibilities that can only be found in the backcountry, in the creek channels and still waters rimmed by mangroves. The Megalopsicle was born out of these fishing situations. It is a neutrally buoyant minnow pattern tied with a spun deer-hair head and craft-fur body. It's designed to track fast and straight. There are times when you are throwing flies to large, wary fish in waters with little or no current to animate the fly, and this is when the Megalopsicle shines. This fly is deadly for snook, tarpon, sea trout, snapper, and redfish.

7: Crazy Charlie

Considered a staple in every bonefish fly box, the Crazy Charlie is one of the best small, flats-style saltwater patterns. This fly was originally designed to mimic small baitfish such as the glass minnow, but over time has developed into a pattern with many slightly different variations, including some great shrimp and small crab imitations. The Crazy Charlie is a sparse fly tied with vinyl rib as the body, calf-tail hair as the "wing" or over-body, and bead-chain eyes to add just enough weight to create a counterbalance to the calf hair, making the fly swim hook point up and snag-free in shallow water.

6: Reefer Mantis

The Texas and Louisiana coasts have introduced the term *backyard exotic* into the vocabulary of fly fishers. Here, along the relatively ignored shorelines and back bays of the Gulf of Mexico, lie amazing

Like a good hound dog, a Reefer Mantis patiently awaits the next hunting trip.

flats fishing opportunities. They're both numerous and accessible. Redfish and sea trout are now mentioned in the same vein as permit and bonefish . . . and for good reason. The mantis shrimp (ironically, not even a shrimp) is a marine crustacean that is an important food source for the gamefish in these waters. The Reefer Mantis is the most suggestive, realistic fly to have with you when you go.

5: Crease Fly

It's called a Crease Fly because the main ingredient is a piece of flat foam folded back over itself (forming a crease) and glued onto the hook shank. The only other significant materials are stick-on eyes and the bucktail and flash material used for the tail. The Crease Fly was first tied for striped bass and bluefish near Long Island, but has been proven on bonito, albacore, Spanish mackerel, jack, and dolphin. Because this fly is open at the front, it is commonly used as a floating popper, but was intended to be fished in currents or on sinking lines. It is incredibly effective either way.

4: Clouser Minnow

This weighted streamer was first tied by Bob Clouser as a smallmouth bass fly, and has won over the hearts and minds of not only every bass fly fisherman, but the salty souls as well. After catching over seventy species of fish on this fly, Lefty Kreh—one of the most famous and respected ambassadors of our sport—wrote, "I consider the Clouser Minnow to be the single-most effective underwater fly to be developed in several decades!" But this isn't Lefty's list, *is it?* It's mine. So it comes in fourth. The Clouser is tied on a good saltwater hook and, besides thread, only has four ingredients: lead dumbbell eyes, Crystal Flash, and two shades of long bucktail. This fly is so popular among streamer fishermen and tiers that it is almost no longer thought of as a pattern but rather as a style of tying.

3: Del's Merkin Crab

Del Brown's Merkin Crab may have landed more permit than anything other than live bait or wooden spear. Everything about this fly design has set the standard and in some way or another influenced every crab fly that has come since. The perfectly crabby oval is achieved by tying multiple chunks of yarn to the side of the heavy hook shank and then trimming them to shape once the fly is finished. With the general shape of the crab achieved, the fly has the needed realism, coupled with the suggestive motion of the webby hackle and rubber legs. Weighted with lead, the Merkin sinks fast to the bottom of the salt flat and is too good to be passed up by an unsuspecting bonefish or permit.

2: Gotcha

If bonefish are the most common and popular saltwater species for fly fishers to chase, then the Gotcha is the most popular and commonly carried fly. It is simple but effective. The Gotcha is a perfect shallow-water streamer, as it is lightweight but still has just enough weight in its bead-chain eyes to turn the hook point up away from the hang-ups at the bottom of the flat. This fly is made using braided Mylar tubing, pearl braid, and subtle craft fur. It comes in a variety of sizes, weights, and colors, and in most combinations resembles a small shrimp.

1: Lefty's Deceiver

Lefty Kreh revolutionized saltwater fly fishing in the late 1950s with his Deceiver streamer pattern. He developed the fly out of frustration with the fouling tendencies of the existing baitfish flies he was using for stripers in Chesapeake Bay. Lefty's Deceiver is tied using multiple feathers off the back, flashy tinsel wrapped forward for the body, and two colors of bucktail (a dark and a light) swept back to form the rest of the body. For good measure there are a few strands of peacock herl over the top, some pieces of red Crystal Flash on the throat to simulate bleeding gills, and a pair of stick-on eyes epoxied into the head. This fly can be tied in any size or color combination and fished as an attractor pattern or as a realistic imitation of a herring, spearing, bunker, alewife, or mullet.

Chapter 20

The Top Ten Alaskan Streamers

Alaska has a long and rich fly-tying history. The feather and fur creations this place has inspired have all the elegant and meticulous English traditions of the classically dressed Atlantic salmon fly crossed with the utilitarian simplicity of the steelheaders on the American West Coast—deposited into the rugged subsistence lifestyle of Alaska. The fishing here has never been difficult. The prime rivers are in remote places accessible only by bush plane, and many of the rest are reliant on salmon runs that introduce a new batch of naive fish into the drainage every year. Mix these rivers of plenty with a long, dark winter and the perfect stage is set for an amazing, fun, and sometimes downright gaudy culture of fly design. But these traditions are being abandoned and replaced by an orange plastic bead threaded onto a leader, trailed by a bare snagging hook. *The pegged egg.* A plastic bead is not a fly because it is not tied. And whereas "angling" is fooling a fish into willingly taking your disguised hook into its mouth, "snagging" is forcing a hook into a fish. If you purposely distance the hook away from the lure object that you are fishing (be it 2 feet or 2 inches) and then *pull the hook into the fish* once it has taken or gotten close to the lure . . . you are snagging fish. That being said, these are the top ten streamers that have influenced a dying genre and are still used by the remaining Alaskan fly fishers.

10: Polar Shrimp

Created in Northern California on the Eel River in the 1930s, the Polar Shrimp is a staple in the fly boxes of West Coast steelheaders and

The Polar Shrimp has been around long enough for our grandparents to have fished it.

Alaskan fly fishers. This fly is a simple suggestion of a dead or dying shrimp tied with the bright, contrasting attractor colors: red, white, and orange.

9: Green Butt Skunk

This is the most well-known steelhead fly pattern ever tied. The Green Butt Skunk was born in Oregon on the North Umpqua River in the 1970s and quickly made the migration up to Alaska. The fly is similar in classic structure as the Polar Shrimp, but is tied with black body chenille and hackle and the distinctive green or chartreuse butt. The Skunk will win the hearts and minds of anything that swims in Alaskan waters.

8: Boss

This is another old West Coast steelhead fly that influenced the tying traditions of Alaska. The Boss is one of the original "comet-style" fly patterns that originated on the Russian River in Northern California back in the late 1940s. This pattern has weight tied on the shank and at the head in the form of bead-chain or dumbbell eyes. Typically the Boss is tied with a black tail and body, with long orange hackle at the front. Intended for steelhead, this fly will also work for every species of Pacific salmon, as well as char and grayling.

7: Killawatte

This fly was conceived on the Salmon River in Idaho in the early 1990s and was extensively fished in the Skeena drainage in British Columbia before being tied commercially. The Killawatte is a black and blue, ultra-flashy steelhead fly tied on a weighted jig hook, and matches the appearance of the spoons used by conventional gear fishermen. It regularly outfishes the classic steelhead patterns and has become an instant favorite in Alaska. Use this fly for steelhead, big stream-resident rainbow trout, char, and all species of Pacific salmon.

6: Articulated Leech

A popular destination area in Alaska is the southwest part of the state where the larger, stream-resident rainbows live. The better rivers in the region are not accessible from the limited road system, so many of these big trout are aggressive, unpressured predators and will chase down the biggest, meanest-looking flies. A black articulated leech streamer has been seen hanging limp and soggy from a gaping mouth in many "fish of the trip" grip-and-grin photos. There are many long, articulated leeches being sold in shops these days and they all look and act the same, so I don't have a favorite. Most are in the 4-inch range, but some of the more wicked-looking ones are double-jointed and over 7 inches long. Go big or go home.

5: Supervisor

This fly was created by Carrie Stevens in 1925 as an attractor streamer that mimicked fingerling smelt, designed for large brook trout in and around Maine. The Lake Supervisor was originally tied with jungle cock and white feather as a "throat" and dominated by green and blue feathers on top as the "wing," capped off with several long peacock herls. I was introduced to this fly by a commercial halibut fisherman I worked for on Kodiak Island. He showed me a modified version of the fly called a Bucktail Supervisor that was tied with a red yarn tail, a silver body, and a sparse wing of bucktail in white, green, and blue. There were a couple peacock strands on top still, but no jungle cock cheeks. This was my skipper's favorite fly, and I saw him land many sockeye salmon from the Buskin River while other fishermen were attempting to floss fish under the false assumption *reds don't eat flies!* This fly pattern is widely accredited to—and named after—a supervisor of fish wardens for the state of Maine. But the real story is that Carrie Stevens created the Supervisor for this fisherman, who *was not* a fly tier.

4: Flesh Fly

"Matching the hatch" is an integral part of successful fly fishing. The term is used in reference to matching your artificial fly pattern to the natural bug seen emerging (and being eaten) off the surface of a trout stream. Recently fly fishers have adopted the phrase to mean matching the fly to *whatever* it is the fish are actively feeding on. If trout or char are back behind a pod of spawning salmon, they are there to eat the eggs whisked loose from the fresh redds, and tying on an egg pattern can be considered *matching the hatch.* I once used split-shot to sink a #4 adult stonefly to fool a big brown trout downstream from a couple kids feeding ducks. The large clump of elk hair used as the fly's wing looked just like a sunken piece of Wonder Bread. *Matching the hatch.* In Alaska most coastal rivers are completely void of life, until a run of salmon move in. These giant waves of fish arrive in a river and provide enough sustenance to take care of all the bears, eagles, and other fishermen that come to the river. The salmon dump their eggs (consumed by the trout and char following the pods upriver) and then die in the water. The rotting salmon carcasses gradually break up and get washed back toward the ocean, creating a chowder-like detritus. Most of the fish flesh never makes it back to saltwater and instead gets trapped in back eddies and wedged between river rocks, providing needed nutrients to the soon-to-be-hatching salmon fry. Flesh flies are then used very effectively to catch any other opportunistic predator that is still in the river—again, *matching the hatch.* Flesh flies are simple patterns consisting most often of a tan strip of rabbit hide wrapped around the hook shank. The tan rabbit fur looks exactly like pale chunks of sashimi. My favorite flesh pattern is the Bandit Leech because it has a band of reddish-orange rabbit tied in the middle. This probably makes no difference to the fish it is intended for, but to me it looks like there might still be some flavor left.

3: Alaskabou

Alaskabou streamers are truly Alaskan-born, last-frontier guide flies. They are simple, sturdy streamers made up of nothing more than brightly colored marabou plumes and Flashabou, and are tied in five color combinations: black-blue, green-white, orange-pink-white, orange-pink-purple, and pink-purple. The Alaskabou evolved from the marabou "spider flies" of the 1970s and turned into a Far North staple because of its simplicity, seductive movement, and varying color options for every fish species and situation.

2: Egg-Sucking Leech

The Egg-Sucking Leech was first experimented with on the streams and rivers around Anchorage and now can be found in almost every fly box in the state. This is basically a large Woolly Bugger streamer with an "egg" tied in as a head. The bright orange or pink head is traditionally tied using chenille, but a colored brass or tungsten bead or even hot-melt glue can be used to add more weight to the fly. The Egg-Sucking Leech is a black or purple streamer with a bright spawn-colored attractor/trigger at the front—*not,* as it's name would imply, an attempt to mimic a leech attached to an egg.

The "egg" in an Egg-Sucking Leech is meant to act as an attractor rather than as a true imitation of an egg.

An attractor like the Flash Fly is always a temptation for larger fish.

1: Flash Fly

The most universal Alaskan streamer is the Flash Fly. Originated on Kodiak Island and commonly called the Karluk Flash Fly, this streamer is made almost entirely of silver Flashabou for the wing and tail and silver diamond braid for the body. Usually the Flash Fly has red saddle hackle at the front, but other colors have been used by Alaskan fly tiers. The effectiveness of this fly has to do with the intense flash and movement of the materials, making it irresistible to large, aggressive fish.

Chapter 21

The Top Ten Beginning Tying Patterns

The two most crippling obstacles most beginning fly tiers set up for themselves are poor equipment and unreasonable ambition (immediately tackling fly patterns that are too complicated for their skill set). A cheap fly-tying vise is never easy or fun to work with, and I know you can't justify throwing down $150 to $300 on a piece of equipment before you know if it is all going to work out for you, but you *can* afford a decent bobbin—this is the culprit behind most of the thread breaking and cursing at the vise. The other problem is overstepping your skill level before you even start. As a beginning tier you have to sit back, be honest with yourself, and pick out the flies you fish the most but that are the easiest to tie and have the least amount of material. At the end of your first two-hour tying session, you are going to have a few very ugly flies in a pile next to you. But the idea is to have them be *functionally* ugly. Start with patterns that are nearly impossible to mess up to a point where they will not work. Then tie a hundred of the same thing. You will essentially "pay for" your new vise and tools, and you will be learning and retaining things, not bouncing around from one poorly tied pattern to another without remembering or accomplishing a thing. This section *will not* teach you how to tie each pattern, but it will tell you why they should be tied.

10: Annelids

These are small aquatic worms that are most often found in fine tailwater substrates. They are also very effective flies. Annelids could be the easiest flies to tie, and you can do them in just about any size you feel good starting with. But only start here if these are flies you already have in your box—no sense in spending time on something you have no intention of ever fishing. Some of the most commonly used Annelida fly patterns are the San Juan Worm, I.E.D., and Pig Sticker. The San Juan Worm is nothing more than a piece of fine pink or red chenille tied onto a curved hook. The I.E.D. and Pig Sticker are only slightly more complicated, but can be achieved with minimal materials, heavy thread, and fairly common hooks.

9: Midge Pupae

A staple in almost every trout's diet because they are plentiful and active year-round, midge pupae are my bread and butter patterns. I tie more of these flies every year than anything else because they are fast to tie, fun to tie, and I fish them more than any other trout fly. Tie your midges on a curved-shank hook like the Tiemco 2488, but start out with some of the larger lake midges. These chironomids, or "buzzers" as they are known in the United Kingdom, are a must-have for any serious lake fisherman and are the perfect introduction or starting block midge pattern. You can perfect your technique on a much larger canvas (a #12 or #14 hook) that you can scale down later. And what you scale down to is the #20 and #22 Zebra Midges, Brassies, and Poison Tungs that utilize very basic tying steps and material but will catch trout anywhere, anytime.

8: Scuds and Sow Bugs

Small crustaceans like scuds and sow bugs are the next logical steps into slightly more complicated fly tying. You may have gotten confident with some of your Poison Tung midges, putting a small tuft of dubbing right behind the bead at the end there. And maybe you got a little crazy with the wire ribbing and flashbacks on some of those big chironomids. So you very likely are all ready to tie a scud. Use a similar-style hook, maybe a #16 Tiemco 2457. Tie in one or two different-colored strands of small wire, some translucent Scud Back or a narrow strip of plastic freezer bag, and then fill the hook up with dubbing. I like Hareline Ice Dub in UV Tan or Light Olive. Brush all the dubbing down and trim to proper leg length, bring the plastic over the top, wrap the wires forward, and POW!

7: PTs and Hare's Ears

Now you are ready to do some multicomponent bugs—nymphs that have tails, abdomens, and thoraxes. You know, bug body parts. Once you get to this point, you should be more in control of the tools and materials so that the subtleties of these can be tweaked and manipulated to get all the correct proportions. Pheasant Tail and Hare's Ear nymphs tied in various sizes and colors can resemble almost any mayfly nymph and almost any small stonefly. Tie a lot of these flies with bead-heads on Tiemco 3769 hooks in #18, #16, and #14. Trust me, you will use them.

6: Ashers and Gnats

You may have noticed that I had you start tying all subsurface flies— this was on purpose. Different types of flies are built to serve a function, and nymphs and pupae are meant to sink. It is easy to build a ship that sinks, but it takes proper minds and hands to build one that can survive an iceberg. But I think you are ready. Orange Ashers, UV Ashers, Griffith's Gnats, and Renegades are all excellent reasons to start using good dry fly saddle feathers. These are very simple patterns that rely on only two or three different materials, and they can fill a midge box quickly. Use Tiemco 100 hooks in a wide range of sizes.

5: Beetles and Ants

Okay, you're cruising along now. Time to throw in some new stuff. This is also a good time to start a conversation about the importance of terrestrials. If you are just starting out as a fly fisher, you have no doubt been pummeled with information about aquatic insects and their life stages and seasonal hatches. It can begin to sound like someone left the door open to science class. But you would be remiss not to devote a portion of your fly box, or of your tying time, to these accidental meal opportunities. Try tying some dubbing-bodied ants and black beetles with peacock herl, a strip of foam, and maybe a pair of rubber legs. Use the same Tiemco 100 dry fly hook you used for the Ashers and Gnats.

4: Para-Mayflies

Now you are ready to tie some *real* dry flies. Start with the basics— parachute hackled mayflies. Tie some larger ones at first, maybe some Adams on a #14 Tiemco 100 hook. The Para-Adams is one of the best and most versatile of all the mayfly imitations because it is slim and suggestive and *kind of* looks like 80 percent of all mayflies across the country. Once you have those knocked out, move down into some smaller dry fly hooks and maybe play around with some slightly different-colored hackle and body dubbing. Tie different species of mayflies—you want your fly boxes to be influenced solely by the waters you fish.

3: Elk Hair Caddis

Tying flies with elk hair can be difficult and frustrating, and that is why I have kept the Elk Hair Caddis from you until you have already done a little of everything else. The body of this fly is easy, because you have essentially already done it when you tied the Ashers. The problems come when you tie in the elk hair wings for the first time.

They will look a tad sloppy at first, and once you get them tidy, they will slide around to the wrong side of the hook shank and then your thread will break. So start with smaller clumps of elk hair, pick out the finer underfur thoroughly, use a heavy brass hair-stacker (not one of those cheap ones), and use thicker thread.

2: Leeches

By now you have conquered all of the minor challenges in trout flies and are ready to move on to more advanced patterns and flashy, new materials. But before you go, tie some simple but deadly trout streamers. Few fish anywhere will turn their nose up at a leech. The easiest and most effective pattern may be the Pine Squirrel Leech. The dyed black strip of squirrel hide about covers it. Hard to mess it up once you have that.

The infamous Woolly Bugger.

1: Woolly Buggers

These streamers can be tied using a wide variety of colors and body materials to emulate leeches, crayfish, and sculpin. During many of my early fly-tying classes, I *started* students on this pattern. The Woolly Bugger is a simple fly, but utilizes almost all of the basic tying techniques. And as it is commonly tied on #4, #6, or #8 nymph hooks (Tiemco 3761), it makes a pleasantly large canvas on which to work and admire mistakes. Also, I like it because a black Bugger is one of my go-to small streamers. But most beginning fly-tying students couldn't care less. They want to tie Copper Johns and Royal Stimulators. So go on now, tie whatever you want—that is, after all, why you learn to tie your own, right?

Chapter 22

The Top Ten Fly-Tying Tricks

Now that I think about it, that is a dumb title for this chapter. There are no *tricks* in fly tying, just better ways of doing things. It does not matter if you intend to tie your first fly sometime tomorrow night, or have worn through so many vises that you can't remember your first. If you are observant and willing, you will never stop learning

Sharpie pens are always handy on a fly-tying desk.

things. I am lucky to be surrounded by an absolute warren of superb fly tiers, including a half dozen of the most talented fly designers in the world. I never pass up an opportunity to watch these tiers in action or compare professional notes. These are the best ten things I have learned.

10: The Right Equipment

I have done many fly-tying demonstrations, and at some point during every one, I will hear someone comment from the back of the room, "He makes it look so easy!" Sure, it feels good to have an ego stroke from time to time, but the reality of the situation is at least half of any

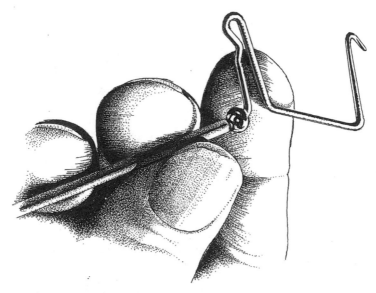

A good Matarelli whip finish tool will save you time and frustration.
Kendall Zimmerman

good tier's talents are a direct result of proper equipment. A world-renowned brain surgeon armed with a plastic cafeteria spork is nothing more than a weird felony assault suspect. If you want to be a good fly tier, you have to spend as much time at the bench as you possibly can, but this alone will not get you all the way there. Treat yourself, don't cheat yourself—buy an expensive Tiemco ceramic bobbin and ask for another every time you feel you have a gift coming your way. And get a good Matarelli whip finish tool. You will own these little gadgets for life, and because they are good quality, they will make that life far less frustrating. It goes without saying you need a decent vise, but more importantly, you need an easy and *permanent* tying area with proper lighting.

9: Get Yourself Organized

You may be surprised at how well and efficiently you tie once you have a tying area that is organized. Creativity is a messy business, I'll grant you, but if you do your best to keep your tools and materials in order, your imagination and budding talents will not be slowed down by futile searches for the last gadwall feather that mysteriously ended up under the tool caddy. Get some Spirit River Utility Boxes with twenty compartments to store your hook collection. Label each box by type of hook (dry fly, nymph, streamer, etc.) and label each compartment by make/model/size. Also, get yourself a set or two of cheap plastic drawers to segregate other materials such as hackle, dubbing, hairs, and flashy stuff.

8: Heavy Thread

You can tie *almost* every fly you need using some of the heaviest thread—you just have to learn to tie with less wraps. Forced moderation is good, and this does whatever you might want done on the hook shank, only faster. Heavy thread can easily lash down thick foam and large clumps of deer or elk hair, as well as build a midge pupa body. Collect an assortment of Danville 6/0 (roughly 70 denier) thread in common colors. Tying without the constant fear of thread breakage is liberating.

7: Do Your Chores

Designing new fly patterns is one thing; tying what you need for tomorrow's fishing or the next guide season is another. You will save untold amounts of time by focusing on one pattern in one size and tying a season's worth. This can be monotonous, but chores usually are. If you bounce back and forth between completely different flies, you will waste a lot of time and make a horrendous mess of your tying bench. I will often "stage tie" many of my more complex fly patterns to save even more time. If there is a natural stopping point or drastic material transition during the construction of a fly, stop there and repeat those first steps on another hook. Don't go back and finish them until you have a few dozen abdomens built. This saves time, but is also a good way to force yourself to crank out that batch of old reliables you *know* you are going to need on the water.

6: Cheap Charlie

No, I am not suggesting that Charlie Craven is a miser. (He has a serious weakness for big-kid toys that make a lot of noise, actually.) It is just a figure of speech. Incorporate as much of the inexpensive tying materials into your designs as you can. Some of the cheapest stuff happens to be the best anyway. Stock up on pheasant tail feathers, peacock herl, marabou in all the natural colors, and as much dubbing in as many colors and consistencies as you can get your hands on. When it comes to hooks, buy the best if you can afford them, but get them in bulk in the sizes and styles you use the most.

5: Avoid the Witches' Brew

This is an odd, sheep-like phenomenon you will gradually notice if you ever spend time on the retail end of fly design. The creative process involved in the design of a new fly pattern is not magic. It is just a solitary craftsman building something new or slightly tweaking something that already exists. This fly tier attempts to build what he has in his head, using whatever materials he has available to him at that very moment. If he feels so inclined, he will document the recipe and maybe even post it on his blog or website. This is when the aspiring tier discovers the Magic Potion while surfing the web, and then scrambles to the nearest fly shop in search of all the exact ingredients: *eye of newt and toe of frog, wool of bat and tongue of dog, adder's fork and blind-worm's sting . . .* These fly tiers will not accept material substitutes even if they will undoubtedly improve the design. It is, after all, a witches' brew and the spell won't work if it is not made just as it was written and the right chants are not sung.

4: The Best Parts Are Body Parts

Most of us are born owning two of the best fly-tying tools ever made. Yeah, *your hands.* The faster you increase your dexterity and learn to fully utilize all ten of your fingers instead of relying on the next wave of new and improved gadgetry, the better off you will be. Stop chewing your fingernails, and don't be afraid to get your tongue involved. Licking your fingers and adding some dampness to some materials like marabou and rabbit fur can make them much more manageable. And discovering your *other* two hands is always a big breakthrough. We all use our index and middle fingers against our thumbs to grasp things, but the other "hands" are your pinkie and ring finger against the palm of your hand.

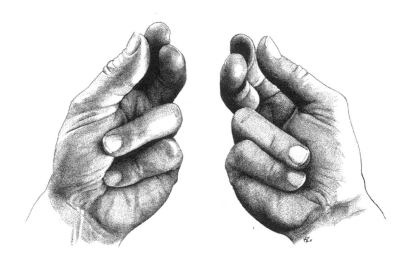

Most of us are born owning two of the best fly-tying tools ever made.
KENDALL ZIMMERMAN

3: Garbage Bag Bears

Have you ever walked down a sidewalk in town and been startled by a group of people in the shop window standing really still and really close to the window? No? Yeah, me neither. None of us ever confuse mannequins with real people. *Ever.* They are proportionally perfect and very realistic. Remember the one that looked like Elaine from *Seinfeld*? We are never duped or startled because our eyes are superb sensory organs and can detect those subtle movements that translate to "something's alive in my peripheral vision!" On the other hand, if you spot a black garbage bag getting tossed around by the breeze down in a roadside ditch in bear country, well, it can add a jolt of adrenaline to your morning jog. It is the right size, right color, and it sure moves like its alive! Keep this philosophy in mind at the vise. Suggestive, lifelike flies with good movement always trump über-realistic but stiff replicas.

2: Be a Good Closer

Finishing a fly soundly has many benefits. Cosmetics are one thing (important to some, not so much to others), but finishing a fly so that it is as durable as possible is important on a purely functional level. You never want to spend time on a fly, no matter how fast and simple it may be, that is bound to unravel and fall apart after one or two fish. A good fly tier will often keep a fly that starts to fall apart on the water. This "injured soldier" should be thoroughly inspected back in the rear (barracks/tying bench) to see what can be done to improve the durability of the pattern. Sometimes the best improvements are really simple: Adding a second whip finish knot and a small dab of head cement will often do the trick.

1: Bathtub Testing

We have an almost daily conversation at the fly shop about new fly designs and ideas (sometimes on the bizarre side if someone left the lid off the jar of Softex). Part of our morning routine, apart from flipping on the lights and the OPEN sign by the front door and getting the coffee going, is dumping the fruits of our previous night's tying labors onto the counter to be perused and criticized by our coworkers. This very honest feedback (sometimes brutally honest) and constructive exchange of theories and ideas is maybe the best perk of working and being fully submersed in the fly-fishing industry. The biggest questions of new flies are always "How does it look in the water?" and "Does it ride right?" The most valuable tool you can have is a test tank. You never want to waste time on more than one prototype if the first fly acts weird or doesn't keel correctly. At the shop we keep a small aquarium full of water for this purpose. At home I use the kitchen sink, or the bathtub. I can only justify filling up the tub if I have a bunch of different prototypes that have already passed the shop tank or sink tests, and I have the time to jump in for a soak when I'm done—a good reason to crimp your barbs, if you were needing one.

Chapter 23

The Top Ten Destinations
in the United States

This chapter is not intended to clue you, the reader, into ten yet undiscovered places to go fly fishing. I will never draw unnecessary attention to a specific body of water that cannot withstand the added pressure my words direct to it, as is the duty of all sports writers. I also don't mean this to be a list of the best places for hard-core anglers to add to their bucket list. What I intend this list to do is offer the budding lunatic a list of places to visit to experience all the different extremes of this sport. I envision a third-year enthusiast who has come to the realization that fly fishing has consumed more brain space and imagination than originally intended, and who is beginning to gaze out past the confines of state lines in search of other opportunities. These ten locations were chosen with very specific styles of fly fishing in mind and based on ease for the do-it-yourselfer, as well as opportunities to roll large if that's more your style.

10: Bozeman, Montana

This is the heart of fly-fishing country. Trout are the keystone of this sport and Montana is the Graceland, no matter how hard any of us try to dodge the subject or argue the point. Bozeman is a city of less than 40,000 people and is the epicenter of everything fly fishing. When you go, focus on the mountain scenery, on the rivers, and on the trout . . . probably the three main hooks that got you strung out on this sport in the first place. There are thousands of streams to see within a half-day's drive of Bozeman, but on your first trip you should experience rivers such as the Gallatin, Yellowstone, and Madison. And don't forget: You'll be less than an hour's drive from Yellowstone National Park. On your return visit you should include one of the famed spring creeks, such as Armstrong's, DePuy's, Nelson's, or Milesnicks. There's some phenomenal dry fly fishing to be had from late April to early May. Runoff in the area peaks from mid-May to mid-July—so avoid this time. Predictably, the best fishing is from early summer into the fall season. Bring a 9-foot, 5-weight rod loaded with floating line and enough slush fund to properly tip your guide if you decide to float with a professional.

9: Cape Cod, Massachusetts

The Cape is the easternmost part of Massachusetts and encompasses fifteen separate small coastal towns, as well as multiple islands just offshore—Martha's Vineyard and Nantucket being the best known. You go to Cape Cod with heavy rod in hand to do one thing: find striped bass. These fish are wily, aggressive, and fight like few things you will ever find yourself attached to, intentionally or otherwise. They are not easy to catch, but the emotional impact the drawn-out act of finding, fishing to, and eventually landing a striper is what fuels the obsession. To be successful as a coastal fly fisherman you will need to pay attention to the weather, the season, and the tides. Plan to go anytime from mid-May to the end of October, but be conscious of Memorial Day/Labor Day–type weekends because the Cape is a popular tourist destination. I recommend finding a guide with a good boat for at least the first day or two, but if you intend to prowl the flats on foot, be careful and be aware of the tide. Bring a 9- or 10-weight rod with a variety of floating, intermediate, and fast-sinking tips. A stripping basket to strap to your waist for collecting loose fly line when you are on the move is also a good idea. The bass you are likely to find will be in the 8- to 10-pound range, but a 40-

or 50-pounder could wreck you at any given moment—leaving you a sniveling and obsession-bitten mess on the beach or boat deck. You may also find bluefish, bonito, and false albacore at certain times of the year in addition to the coveted striper. Take 9-foot leaders in the 10- to 20-pound class and maybe some 30- to 50-pound shock tippet if you are going to be offshore and have a chance at some bigger fish. The favorite flies for the area are Deceivers, Reducers, Super and Flashfire Mushies, Magnum Baitfish, and Magic Squid.

8: Guntersville, Alabama

Guntersville is a town of less than 8,000 people on the shore of the state's largest and most reputable bass lake. Guntersville Lake is 69,000 acres of countless grassy bays and shallows and 950 miles of shoreline. If you own a boat and trailer, by all means drag it down with you, as this is certainly not a half-acre farm pond, but there are guide outfits in town who would love to have you out for a day or two. The best time to be there is late March through early June, before the dense milfoil beds get too thick and the water temps rise and push the bass deep and out of easy reach of most fly anglers. Don't hesitate to check out other lakes nearby if you are staying longer. Wheeler Lake (part of the Tennessee River) is only 40 miles away and at 67,000 acres is the second-largest lake in Alabama. The average bass is not as large as what you will find in Guntersville, but you will undoubtedly land more fish. For a different experience, try Smith Lake. This lake is 50 miles from Guntersville and is smaller (21,200 acres) but clearer and significantly deeper (over 200 feet in places). Focus on the shorelines and around prominent structures. You will find plenty of largemouths and an equal number of closely related spotted bass. And there are striped bass prowling this lake that are significantly larger than the largemouth bass. Bring stiff 7- or 8-weight rods with floating and sink-tip lines with very stout leaders.

7: Hayward, Wisconsin

The reason you go to Wisconsin is to pit yourself and your puny buggy whip of a fly rod against the most predatory and vicious fish in freshwater: *muskellunge*. There are decent brown trout in the Namekagon River and the fly fishing there can be quite fun from April through late June, and you can have great days in June and July fishing streamers to big smallmouth bass (6 to 7 pounds), but that's not when you are going to go, or why you are going to go. Again, it is the muskie. And it will be in October and November. Big muskie. So take your 8-, 9-, or 10-weight rods, fat floating lines, and big baitfish streamers. There are countless lakes and rivers in and around the small town of Hayward (less than 3,000 people) and the nearby 850,000-acre Chequamegon National Forest. You could spend a lifetime or two exploring these waters on your own, but given a week or ten days, hire a guide to take you out. There are outfitters in town who cater specifically to fly anglers.

6: Key Largo, Florida

Hop a flight to Miami, and a short drive later you're out of the city and in the backyard of whatever quarry you want. Everglades National Park has a plethora of freshwater streams and ponds with large Florida-strain largemouth bass, and the canal systems in and around Miami hold a lot of both peacock bass and largemouth bass in the 14- to 17-inch range. You may stumble onto a small snook or tarpon in these canals as well—which can really keep things interesting. At night you can loiter around the lighted docks and find snapper, mackerel, sea trout, ladyfish, and jacks. But the real reasons a fly fisher goes to Florida (and the Key Largo area specifically) are for the labyrinth-like backcountry and the massive flats. Getting to these areas is very difficult to impossible if you are on your own and without watercraft. To take full advantage of this ultimate and diverse

Dave Student with a Florida Keys tarpon. GREG FRIEDMAN

fishing experience, hire a guide for a day or two. In the back bays and among the mangroves you will find tarpon, snook, redfish, and sea trout, and on the flats there will be tarpon, bonefish, jacks, and permit . . . and, for better or worse, sharks and barracuda. And they will all take a fly and then do their best to destroy you.

This area has been able to offer fly anglers a quality education in saltwater fishing despite the dense population and fishing pressure because the extensive flats and shallow cover (within close proximity to the Gulf Stream and deeper water) translate to a tremendous amount of food for gamefish. Plan your trip for early in the year (April through June), but if you can get there in May, you will have the best shot at all the most desired species. For bonefish, bring an 8- or 9-weight fly rod, floating line, and 9- to 10-foot, 8- to 12-pound leaders. For permit and baby tarpon, bring a 9- or 10-weight rod with floating line (maybe a second line with a slow sink-tip) and 10- to 12-foot, 12- to 16-pound leaders. For the big tarpon (80 to 150 pounds), bring an 11- or 12-weight rod, floating line, 16- to 20-pound leaders with 40- to 80-pound shock tippet, and a big reel with a superb drag and 300 yards of backing.

5: Kodiak, Alaska

The Alaskan species usually focused on by venturing fly fishers are king salmon, silver salmon, and big resident rainbows. The obstacle in pursuing any of these esteemed fish is your being only one of thousands of other fishermen fighting over the same riverbank, or having to spend *a lot* of money getting to a remote river where you don't have to play well with others. This is precisely why I'm directing you to Kodiak Island—it's off the beaten path enough to allow for solitude on the water even within the easily accessible road system, but has superb remote locations for those who have the means and motivation to pay a bush pilot to take them and leave them to the mercy of the bears. Because it is an island, Kodiak has no rivers long enough to get very wide or deep, giving the novice angler a fighting chance to learn how to swing a fly without *too much* extended futility. I recommend visiting the island during the semi–off-time at the very end of August when the rivers are brimming with 3- to 6-pound pink salmon and the first of the big silvers have just begun to enter the river . . . and they will be chrome and fresh from the salt, sea lice still attached. The silver salmon won't be up in force until September, but with the peak of this salmon run comes the influx of fishing tourists. The population of the island can temporarily double during the silver salmon run. A 9½-foot, 7-weight rod with a 5- to 8-foot sink-tip line and short 10-pound leader may be the ideal Kodiak setup. A sink-tip line is crucial to get a swinging fly to the proper depth. The rivers may be short and not too wide, but the currents are swift.

4: Lander, Wyoming

Lander is a true western town of 7,000 people right at the edge of the Bridger-Teton National Forest (3.4 million acres), the Shoshone National Forest (2.4 million acres), and the 3,500-square-mile Wind River Indian Reservation. You are going there with waders packed and rods at the ready for very obvious reasons. Plan to rent a car, buy a state fishing license as well as a tribal trespass license for the reservation, book a daylong guided float trip down the Wind River Canyon below Boysen Reservoir, and, if you have the legs and back, take a multiple-day backpacking trip into the Wind River Mountains. There are an absolute ton of high, remote lakes as well as small streams and rivers apart from the Wind River itself, full of browns, rainbows, brookies, cutthroats, and some very good-size golden trout. The largest fish of your trip (5 pounds and over . . . *maybe?*) will most likely come from the float through the Wind River Canyon. But don't neglect the Popo Agie, Little Popo Agie, Red Creek, Sweetwater River, and Bull Lake Creek on the days between your hikes and floats. The best times to go will be from July (after the June runoff) all the way through October. Be sure to break in your new hiking boots and a comfortable backpack. Take a 9-foot, 4-weight rod for the small rivers and high lakes, as well as a stiffer, 5- or 6-weight rod for the float on the Wind River. There will be no need for anything other than floating line and a big box of dry flies.

3: Maupin, Oregon

Maupin is the best little town in steelhead country you've never heard of. A short drive from both the hassle and convenience of Bend and Portland, it is a town of only 500 people, smack dab on the bank of the Deschutes River. As a fly fisher, you are on your way to this part of the country to do two things: learn to spey cast and find steelhead. *Real steel.* Big, bright ocean fish that come up the Columbia River and make the hard right turn up the famed Deschutes. These will be 5- to 15-pound fish with the promise of something a bit bigger. The Deschutes has an active "summer run" of steelhead. They will be in the river from July to November, but the best time to be there is September and October. The river is wide, so don't go unless you have the proper gear and are willing to learn to cast the long rod. A 13-foot, 7-weight spey rod will do just fine. Bring floating line as well as some sink tips. There are multiple fly shops in town with guide services that offer both wade and float trips. Use them, if only for their oars and casting advice.

2: New Orleans, Louisiana

Not that you needed another reason to plan a trip to New Orleans, right? The culture, the nightlife, the great Cajun food . . . and big redfish, nose down, tailing in the flats. Your guide will pole the flats boat quietly into casting range (20 feet closer than you said you could cast at the dock that morning). You make the cast—despite your shaking hands—give the fly a moment to sink, and then strip twice. The big tail protruding from the water will disappear and the 10-pound red will pounce on your fly. Are you ready? The Mississippi River sediments dump into the ocean, forming the Louisiana Delta and creating extensive mudflats that become incredible sight-fishing grounds for the fly angler. You will find speckled trout, black drum, and snapper, but the main prize is the abundant 5- to 15-pound redfish. They will be actively feeding in shallow water (3 feet and under) and will aggressively charge and eat a fly. There's a chance of finding fish at any time of the year, but late season is the best as well as most comfortable climate-wise. Plan your trip for the fall, and bring a stiff 9-foot, 8-weight rod with floating line and 9-foot, 13- to 15-pound leaders.

1: Steamboat Springs, Colorado

An underrated aspect of Colorado fly fishing is its diversity. Most freshwater fish species can be found somewhere in the state and are actively pursued. If Colorado is the angler's buffet, then Steamboat Springs is a sampler platter big enough to feed a family. The main attraction is the Yampa River, which flows right through town. You can hire a guide to float you down the Yampa, or you can finish your after-dinner drinks on the back patio of one of the many fine eateries and stroll down to a good run. If you want the big-fish tailwater experience, you can fish the Yampa River below the Stagecoach Reservoir dam. The reservoir itself holds some of the state's largest northern pike, too. Bring an 8-weight rod and some big pike streamers. Steamboat is located next to the Medicine Bow–Routt National Forest, which has countless small trout streams, including Sarvis, Harrison, and Mad Creeks—although the headwater of the Yampa (known as Bear River) is maybe the most fun and overlooked stream in the area. Some excellent lakes are sprinkled about, too—like Bear, Dumont, Crosho, and Pearl—and, in addition to some good-size Colorado River cutthroat trout, there are some Alaska-caliber arctic grayling. Bring a 9-foot, 5-weight rod with floating line and have fun!

Acknowledgments

There are many people I need to thank for making not only this book, but my life in fly fishing possible. Thank you Chet and Monica Cross for welcoming me into the Rocky Mountain Anglers family and allowing me the ability to keep chasing down this dragon. Thank you Randy Hicks for covering for me as I typed for days on end at the back of the fly shop. Thank you Van Rollo and Nick Gibb for your support and good words. Thank you Bruce Olson and Brian Schmidt for playing along with my creative endeavors . . . and for always squeezing the best out of me.

Thank you Dad for showing me how to fish, despite my young attempts to send everything you own to the bottom of the Huron boat basin. Thank you Mum for loving me, believing in me, and always lending your ear and shoulder. Thank you Eva for being a tough big sister and for teaching me how to throw a punch. Thank you Merlot for being my best friend and roommate through the most trying years of my life.

Thank you Frank Smethurst, Dick Orr, Larry Jurgens, and Bob Detling for your weekly visits and never-ending wisdom. Thank you Todd Hosman, Jim Pruett, and Gordon Wickstrom for years of reading the silly things I write and continuing to encourage me to write more. Thank you Patrick Knackendoffel for being the only human able to keep "the byrd" reined in. Thank you Joe Novosad for vouching for me and Allen Jones for giving me this job. Thank you Charlie Craven, Rob Kolanda, and John Gierach for your friendship, professional advice, and inspiration. Thank you A. K. Best, Tom Macy, Cliff Watts, and Chris Schrantz for your help and for your stories. Thank you Mike Kruise and Steve Schweitzer for your camaraderie and encouragement.

But, most of all . . . thank you Erin Block. You are the best fishing partner I could ever have on this, or any other river.

Index

(Italicized page numbers indicate illustrations.)

Adams, Charles, 111
Alaskabous (streamers), 145–46
American-made equipment, 7–8, 14
Amy's Ants (flies), 108–9
anchor nymphs, 64
anglers, other, 75, 85. *See also* partners, fishing
Annelids (tying pattern), 149–50
ants (tying pattern), 152
arbor sizes, 12–13
Articulated Leeches (streamers), 143–44
ashers (tying pattern), 151
attitude, 100
Autumn Splendors (streamers), 120

Backstabbers (flies), 129
Bandit Leeches (streamers), 145
Banksia Bugs (nymphs), 114, *115*
barbless hooks, 63, 84, 87
beer, 46
Beetles (flies), 111
beetles (tying pattern), 152
Belly Ache Minnows (streamers), *123,* 123–24
boat etiquette, 82
Booby Frogs (flies), *130,* 130–31
boots and waders, 25–32, *26, 51,* 82
Boss (streamers), 143

boxes, fly, 35, *36,* 49, 157
Bozeman, Montana, 163–64
brands, 6, 14–15, 22
Brown, Del, 139
buzzers, 150

capacity, 9–10
Cape Cod, Massachusetts, 164–65
casting
    novice mistakes in, 96
    rod selection and, 5–6
    techniques and tips for, 80, 89–94
catch-and-release, 83
cell phones, 39
Charlie's Airheads (flies), 128
Chili Pepper Worms (flies), 136
chironomids, 150
"clean up" (partner maneuver), 76
clothing, 31, 77, 96
Clouser, Bob, 138
Clouser Minnows (flies), 132–33, 138
Clown Shoe Caddises (flies), 107–8, *108*
Comparaduns (flies), 110–11
coolers, soft, 37
Copper Johns (nymphs), 114, 154
courtesy, 45, 81–85
Crazy Charlies (flies), 137
Crease Flies (flies), 138
cross training, 70
Curmudgeon Crumplers (flies), 109–10, *110*

Dahlberg's Divers (flies), 131–32
Deeter, Kirk, 89–90
DeLorme Atlas & Gazetteer, 38–39
Del's Merkin Crabs (flies), 139
destinations, 163–71
details, attention to, 69–70
Doctor, Garrison, *101*
double hauls, 93
double uni knots, *56, 57*
drag, 12
Drummond, Tim, 77
dry and dropper rigs, 61–62
dry fly fishing rigs, single, 61
ducks, 74

eastern nymphing, 63
education, 41, 97
Egg-Sucking Leeches (streamers),
    146, *146*
Elk Hair Caddises (flies), 111, 152–53
ethics, 43
etiquette, 45, 81–85
Euro-nymphing rigs, 63–64
exaggeration, 83

fish
    photographing, 105–6
    respect for, 85–87, *86*
    things that scare, 77–78
fishermen and fisherwomen, other,
    75, 85. *See also* partners, fishing
fishing technique improvement tips,
    67–70, 72, 79–80
fitness, 67

Flash Flies (streamers), 147, *147*
Flashtail Whistlers (flies), 128
Flesh Flies (streamers), 144
flies
    Alaskan streamers, 141–47, *142,
        146, 147*
    for information trade, 46
    saltwater, 135–40, *137*
    trout dry, 107–12, *108, 110, 112*
    trout nymphs, 113–18, *115, 116*
    trout streamers, 119–25, *121, 123*
    tying patterns for, 149–54, *153*
    warm-water, 127–33, *130, 132*
    wet *vs.* dry, 64–65
fly threaders, 33–34
fly-tying
    learning to, 48, 68
    patterns for, 149–54, *153*
    tricks for, *155,* 155–62, *156, 160*
food, 52
furled leaders, 20–21

Geezus Lizards (flies), 128
Girdle Bugs (nymphs), 113
glasses, 37–38, 49
gnats (tying pattern), 151
Gotchas (flies), 139
Gray Ghosts (streamers), 119–20
Green Butt Skunks (streamers), 142
Griffith's Gnats (tying pattern), 151
guides, 43, 44, 62, 68–69
Guntersville, Alabama, 165

Halladay, Leonard, 111–12

handling fish, 85–87, *86*
hands, as fly-tying tools, 159, *160*
Hare's Ears (tying pattern), 151
hauls, 92–93
Hayward, Wisconsin, 166
headlamps, 35
Hicks, Randy, *1, 26*
high-stick nymphing, 62–63
hooks, 63, 78–79, 84, 87
Humphreys, Joe, 92

I.E.D. (fly pattern), 150
improved clinch knots, *58,* 59
indicator nymphing rigs, 62

journaling, 69
Jujubaetises (nymphs), 115–16, *116*

Karluk Flash Flies (streamers), 147
Key Largo, Florida, 166–68
Killawatts (streamers), 143
knots
    double uni, *56,* 57
    fear of, as novice mistake, 98–99
    improved clinch, *58,* 59
    loop or drop loop, 59
    nail, 55
    Rapala, 59, *60*
    tippet-to-fly, 57–58, 59
Kodiak, Alaska, 168–69
Kreh, Lefty, 139

lake *vs.* river rigging techniques,
    59, 61

Lander, Wyoming, 169
leaders
    lake *vs.* river rigging for, 59, 61
    rigging techniques for, 57
    selection tips, 20–22
    self-made, as money-saving tip, 48
    tippet spool tenders for
        organizing, 35, 37
leader to tippet rigging technique, 57
"leapfrog" (partner maneuver), 76
leeches (tying pattern), 153
Lefty's Deceivers (flies), 139–40
lines, fly, 17–20, 21–23, 49–50, *50,*
    91–92
lining a fly reel rigging technique,
    53, 55
littering, 85
locations, 47, 72, 81–82, 163–71
LOFT (Lack of Talent), 99–100
loop knot, 59
lunches, 52

maps, 38–39
Matarelli whip finishing tools,
    156, 157
Maupin, Oregon, 169–70
Meat Whistles (flies), 129
Megalopsicles (flies), 136
Micro Mays (nymphs), 117
midge pupae (tying pattern), 150
Missing Links (flies), 109
money-saving tips, 47–52
Muddler Minnows (streamers),
    124–25

nail knots, 55
Near Nuff Crayfishes (flies), 129–30
Near Nuff Sculpins (streamers),
    122–23
Neiswander, Kevin, *11*
net releases, magnetic, 33
New Orleans, Louisiana, 170–71
noise, 78
novice mistakes, 95–100
nymph fishing, 62–64
nymphs
    for Euro-nymphing rigs, 64
    trout, 113–18, *115, 116*

Orange Ashers (tying pattern), 151
organization, 52, 157
over casting, 93–94
over-lining, 20

Parachute Adamses (flies),
    111–12, *112*
para-mayflies (tying pattern), 152
partners, fishing, 68–69, 75–76,
    102, 105
Pheasant Tails (nymphs), 118, 151
photography, 42, 101–6
Pig Sticker (fly pattern), 150
Pine Squirrel Leeches (streamers),
    125, 153
Platte River Spiders (streamers),
    121–22
polarization, 37–38
Polar Shrimps (streamers),
    141–42, *142*

Princes (nymphs), 116
punctuality, 81

Rainbow Warriors (nymphs), 114
Rapala knot, 59, *60*
redd raiding, 84
Reducers (flies), 135–36
Reefer Mantises (flies), *137,* 137–38
reels, fly, 9–15, 11
Renegades (tying pattern), 151
resale of equipment, 51
research, 41, 97
rigging techniques
    dry and dropper, 61–62
    Euro-nymphing, 63–64
    high-stick nymphing, 62–63
    indicator nymphing, 62
    lake *vs.* river, 59, 61
    leader to tippet, 57
    lining a fly reel, 53, 55
    single dry fly, 61
    streamer and wet fly fishing,
        64–65
    tippet to fly, 57–58, 59
river *vs.* lake rigging techniques,
    59, 61
rods, fly, 1–8, 68, 91, 103–4
RS2 (Rim's Semblance 2), 109

San Juan Worms (fly pattern), 150
scuds (tying pattern), 150–51
Sculpzillas (streamers), 120, *121*
setting the hook, 78–79
shadows, 78

Sharpie pens, *155*
shops, fly, 41–46
"sides" (partner maneuver), 76
silhouettes, 78
single dry fly rigs, 61
sinking fly lines, 19–20
sow bugs (tying pattern), 150–51
Sparkle Minnows (streamers), 122
speed, line, 92–93
Spirit River Utility Boxes, 157
split-shot dispensers, 34–35
spooking fish, 77–78
spools, 15, 35, 48
Steamboat Springs, Colorado, 171
Stevens, Carrie, 120, 144
stewardship, 85
Stimulators (flies), 107
streamers
    Alaskan, 141–47, *142, 146, 147*
    rigging techniques for, 64–65
    trout, 119–25, *121, 123*
Student, Dave, *167*
sunglasses, 37–38, 49, 104
Supervisors (streamers), 144
"switch" (partner maneuver), 76

Texas Ringworms (flies), 131, *132*
thread, fly-tying, 157–58
tight-line nymphing, 63
tippets, 57
tippet spool tenders, 35, 37
tippet-to-fly knots, 57–58, 59
tricks of the trade, 73–80
tuber hatches, 73–74
tuck casts, 92
Twenty Inchers (nymphs), 116
Two-Bit Hookers (nymphs), 117–18

waders, 25–32, *26,* 51, 82
warranties, 8, 11, 25, 27
water depth, 79
wet fly fishing rigs, 64–65
Woolly Buggers (streamers), 124,
    153, 154

Zebra Midges (nymphs), 117
Zimmerman, Eva, *71*
Zug Bugs (nymphs), 116

About the Author

Jay Zimmerman has worked as an archaeologist, infantry paratrooper, commercial halibut fisherman, hunting guide (Alaska and Canada), and carpenter. He is currently a fly-fishing guide; fly-tying instructor; comanager of the Rocky Mountain Anglers fly shop in Boulder, Colorado; a Loon Outdoors Ambassador; a commercial fly designer for Umpqua Feather Merchants; and the writer and producer of the popular fly-fishing blog, Colorado Fly Fishing Reports. Jay also maintains his own YouTube channel wherein he publishes short fishing and fly-tying videos.

ERIN BLOCK